WHAT OTHERS ARE SAYING

Anything Andrea Schwartz writes is based on real experience and a profound understanding and love of our religious traditions. As a homeschooler she knows first-hand the vital role family life plays in rearing happy, productive children who will be able to cope with the challenges all Americans are going to face in the decades ahead.

Sam Blumenfeld, *author and educator*

Andrea Schwartz is a vital part of our Christian community. Whether it's organizing and speaking at events, writing, mentoring, or recording podcasts, she is always busy fulfilling her role as a Titus 2 woman. Her mentorship has proved invaluable in teaching young women the hows and whys of Biblical womanhood, parenting, and home education. I am so grateful to have Andrea as a friend and hope that many others will follow her example in rising up to take dominion for Christ by helping and teaching younger women for the glory of God.

Colin Gunn, *filmmaker and homeschooling father*

The world says children happen to you…The Christian family says children are a much bigger part of God's blessing and Providence. Andrea's wise counsel has guided and equipped countless women, including myself, to trust God, see His hand at work and look to Him for His help in parenting. You will be both convicted and blessed by this book.

Rosemarie B., *wife and homeschooling mother of five*

Andrea's ability to make insightful analysis, draw out Biblical wisdom, and offer meaningful applications to many contemporary issues is a rare gift. Reading her materials has proved to be, time and time again, a blessed treat. Here is another sterling example of her tireless efforts to consecrate every area of life for the glory of God.

Rev. Dave B., *homeschooling father of six*

Andrea Schwartz is passionate about teaching others to live Christ-centered lives with common sense and responsibility. Through her insightful books, she encourages her community to weigh everything (parenting, homeschooling, etc.) against God's Word. She offers a wealth of practical life experiences and reflections as encouragement to those who take to heart Proverbs 3:6 and wish to do His will over their own.

Cara G., wife and homeschooling mother of three

Andrea seats her readers in a theological reconstruction class by restating the absoluteness of God's Word and upholding its effectual counsels. With this in mind, readers, parents in particular, will be inspired by her practical examples and grow mature in their parenting.

Linda C., wife and homeschooling mother of three

Andrea's insights, honesty, commitment to the Word of God and its practical application, have been immensely helpful as I have attempted to navigate the sometimes murky and unpredictable waters of homeschooling. Not only do I enjoy reading her books, but I reference them often.

Gloria H., wife and homeschooling mother of five

Andrea's insights on what the Bible has to say about familial relationships and childrearing will not only challenge you to a higher and more God-fearing standard of parenting, but also inspire you to find comfort in the sufficiency of the Scripture and the sovereignty of God.

Elena C., daughter

WOMAN
of the HOUSE

A Mother's Role in Building a Christian Culture

ANDREA SCHWARTZ

Chalcedon / Ross House Books
Vallecito, California

*This book is dedicated to
Dorothy Faith Schwartz*

Other books by Andrea Schwartz

LESSONS LEARNED FROM YEARS OF HOMESCHOOLING
*A Christian Mother Shares Her Insights from a
Quarter Century of Teaching Her Children*

THE HOMESCHOOL LIFE
Discovering God's Way to Family-Based Education

THE BIBLICAL TRUSTEE FAMILY
Understanding God's Purpose for Your Household

TEACH ME WHILE MY HEART IS TENDER
Read Aloud Stories of Repentance and Forgiveness

Contents

Introduction

In a culture that embraces youth, it is not easy to be a Titus 2 Woman. When the Apostle Paul instructs the "older" women to teach the younger ones to love their husbands and children (i.e., become a Proverbs 31 wife), he doesn't use some euphemistic title to get around the fact that he is addressing mature mothers and grand-mothers.

Scripturally speaking, there is no shame in getting older. In fact, Proverbs 16:31 celebrates the "hoary head" as being worthy of honor. What's more, the psalmist in Psalm 71:17–18, while proclaiming God as the rock of salvation, adds,

> O God, You have taught me from my youth;
> And to this day I declare Your wondrous works.
> *Now also when I am old and grayheaded,*
> O God, do not forsake me,
> Until I declare Your strength to this generation,
> Your power to everyone who is to come. [Emphasis added.]

Years ago when I was tempted to cover the gray hairs that began to appear in the midst of my dark brown hair, my husband's remark, "I like your gray hair and I don't want you to cover it," gave me a genuine opportunity to submit to his wishes and model for my daughters that I *walked my talk.* Today, I'm amused that so many want to know where I get my highlights done as my hair color is rightly categorized as salt and pepper, with salt dominating the mixture. Not only does this hair color serve me in good stead because I don't spend time and money trying to reverse the clock, I find it opens the door for younger women to safely confide in me and enter into a mentoring relationship.

The essays in this book represent an effort to declare the strength of Jesus Christ and His law-word in this gray-headed season of my life. They deal with topics important to furthering the Biblical trustee family such as: marriage, childbirth, child-rearing, Christian home education, and sanctified living. My goal is to strengthen the Biblical family by strengthening its members and, in the process, bring glory to the Lord Jesus Christ.

I

Dispelling the Myth that God is a Buttercup

*B*ack in 1984, a friend introduced my husband and me to the writings of R. J. Rushdoony. It wasn't until 1985 that we actually met Rush and started making monthly trips to Vallecito, CA. In getting to know Rush and his wife, Dorothy, we also became friends with the rest of their family, members of the Chalcedon staff, and Chalcedon's resident scholar, Otto Scott.

Otto was in a special category all his own. His grasp of history, his knowledge of world events, and his self-educated style made him a bit intimidating at first. I had to *work* while reading his articles and books and listening to him converse. Otto wasn't about spoon-feeding his readers. He assumed that if you were reading something he wrote, you were interested. He didn't try to make you interested.

Otto used an expression that has become his signature quote, and it is a distillation of a profound Scriptural truth: *God is no buttercup.* Jack Phelps, pastor of Covenant Bible Church, shared in a tribute to Otto after his death in 2006:

> [Otto] spent the dark years of World War II serving with the Merchant Marine, making several perilous crossings of the Atlantic during that conflict. He was on convoy in a North Sea storm, under threat of German attack, when, he said, the fierce forces of nature first caused him to realize that "God is no buttercup!"[1]

---

1   http://www.covenantbiblechurch.com/2012/02/28/otto-scott-a-tribute/, accessed 10-4-12

To be honest, this statement used to irritate me when I heard it, mostly because I didn't really understand why others thought it so special. But as time, maturity, and sanctification have progressed in my life, those words ring truer and truer, and I appreciate their implication.

Randy Booth comments on Otto's buttercup quote,

> Another way to make this point is to recognize that the Bible is not a collection of "precious moments." God's Word speaks to the real world and it makes no apology for doing so. It is filled with stories about a fallen world and its redemption. There are no subjects that are off limits. Some people are embarrassed over certain things in the Bible, but God is not embarrassed. He covers the range of human sin and redemption. He freely speaks of life and death, sex and violence, treachery and warfare, and He does so in graphic terms (e.g., Ezek. 23:17–21; Mal. 2:3). He is not being gratuitous, and neither should we be.
>
> The church should speak more, not less about these "forbidden" subjects. The silence of the church has given us the culture that is around us. If we don't set forth what God says about these things, both in their sinfulness and in their righteousness, then the world will speak to them for us. They will define justice and sexuality and marriage and every other issue.[2]

Yet, in most of today's churches, pastors and congregants busily try to soften the words of a politically incorrect God. The last thing most Christians want from Christian teaching or preaching is an "unkind" view of God, or to be presented with a God who requires obedience to His law-word. God is often portrayed as Someone whose sole purpose is to serve man and make him happy. Of course, these standards are man-centered.

Romans 10:14–17 states:

> *How then shall they call on him in whom they have not believed? and how shall they believe in him of whom they have*

---

not heard? and how shall they hear without a preacher? And how shall they preach, except they be sent? as it is written, How beautiful are the feet of them that preach the gospel of peace, and bring glad tidings of good things! But they have not all obeyed the gospel. For Esaias saith, Lord, who hath believed our report? So then faith cometh by hearing, and hearing by the word of God.

The prevailing theology of the day has transformed the gospel of peace and glad tidings into a message that leads those who hear it to believe they need to make very few changes in their lives. This seeker-friendly church paradigm, which has been our modern evangelistic model, self-consciously chose to do away with more difficult passages of the Bible. It is as though the church finds God's total revelation of Himself an embarrassment and an impediment to the church.

Bojidar Marinov, an international missionary, recently reminded us that changed people change cultures.[3] Those who have been changed by the Holy Spirit, though imperfect, cannot help but be salt and light to those around them. But if church goers have only been fed "baby-food" (Heb. 5:12–14) from the time of their new birth, should we be surprised that their "stomachs" reject meat?

PLEASE, NO BAD NEWS

What is the effect of one generation failing to pass on the "meat of the Word" to the next? Those fed a milk-toast faith do not have the strength to face the trials of life. They have not been taught to seek wisdom and solace from the entire Word of God. They cannot be cultural leaders who apply Biblical solutions to their lives or to a decadent culture. When we see that the alleged divorce rate for professing Christians is identical to that in the general population, and that many church-going women are obtaining abortions, it is obvious that

---

3   In a recent Law & Liberty podcast of the Chalcedon Foundation: http://chalcedon.edu/blog/2011/7/22/law-and-liberty-podcast-bojidar-marinov-translating-rushdoony-and-missions/

the culture is having more impact on the church than the church is having on the culture.

The church today prefers the "buttercup" God over the God of the Bible. I have heard more times than I care to recall that we must not preach a "harsh" God—a God who is angry at sin. There are actually believers who think that sharing the truth that God hates sin will "turn people off" and cause them to flee from Jesus, not flee to Him. Not only does this give man more power than he presumptuously assumes, but it means God needs a public relations firm to deal with the unpleasant parts of His resumé!

The cross is extremely offensive, and intentionally so. God's righteous wrath on the sons of disobedience caused a sinless man to die a horrendous death. And, to add insult to injury, if a person fails to believe and receive the substitutionary atonement provided by the God/Man and thereby submit to His law-word, there is eternal death in store for him. Can we get any more offensive?

But a majority of parents, pastors, and "pleasers" want to take the offense out of the cross and replace it with a *better life now* message. Contrast this with Ephesians 5:6–7:

> *Let no one deceive you with empty words, for because of these things the wrath of God comes upon the sons of disobedience. Therefore do not become partners with them.*

Too many mothers and fathers *have* become partners with the sons of disobedience by telling their children Bible stories rewritten to accommodate a buttercup-God. So, the story of Noah's ark morphs into a story about an old man and his happy wife and friendly animals hanging out of a merrily bobbling-along houseboat. You would never guess it was originally the historical account of a worldwide, catastrophic flood brought upon all creation because of man's un-repented sin resulting in death for all mankind, except the eight souls in the ark. The problem with presenting the Biblical accounts with watered-down versions like this is that we end up believing these fantasies ourselves.[4]

---

4   In my read-aloud story book *Teach Me While My Heart is Tender*, each story conveys the ugly reality of sin, the beauty of godly repentance, and the necessity of forgiveness. Sugar-coating or minimizing sin only serves to vaccinate children from ever seeing

Genesis 6:6–7 says,

> *And the LORD was sorry that He had made man in the land,*
> *and He was grieved in His heart. And the LORD said, "I will*
> *blot out man whom I have created from the face of the land,*
> *from man to animals to creeping things and to birds of the*
> *sky; for I am sorry that I have made them."*

That's what you call an internal commentary from the book of Genesis that identifies God's "motive" for judgment. One might imagine a "kinder/gentler" approach with something like:

> *And the LORD was slightly disturbed that he hadn't made*
> *man as well as he should and was trying to forgive himself for*
> *his bad design.*
> *And the LORD said, "I will give man a time out, as I re-*
> *evaluate my commandments and see if I've been too harsh*
> *with them."*

Passage after passage in Scripture identifies God's utter hatred for violations of His law. Psalm 5:4–6 and Proverbs 6:16–19 are but two.

CULTURE CHANGING PREREQUISITES

The family is the primary God-ordained institution, and any cultural transformation must begin there. As I point out in "Rethinking Child-birth" (Chapter 6), it is advantageous for a woman to experience the travail of labor so that she transitions from carrying her child to mothering her child, thereby becoming *invested* through her own blood, sweat, and tears. The focus necessary to deal with the intensity of labor is excellent preparation for the perseverance needed for a mother to guide her child through the ordeals of infancy and childhood.

Without question, raising children involves dealing with lots of problems since sinfulness is bound up in the heart of a child. The

---

their need for Christ's atonement.

mother is uniquely positioned to teach her children that *life has its share of problems* and how to deal with them in a godly, righteous fashion. If she fears God and keeps His commandments, her witness will be stronger than her words.

R. J. Rushdoony states,

> Childhood, youth, middle age, and old age all have their problems, as does every era of history. Problems are a part of life in a fallen world, and they are a necessary part of it, necessary to our testing and to our growth. Be sure of this: when you solve one problem, you create a new situation which has problems of its own. Problems are in part a product of sin and in part a condition of growth.
>
> We need to accept problems and testing as a condition of life. Even in Eden, apart from the problems of farming, Adam and Eve were every day put to the test. The tree of the knowledge of good and evil could be bypassed or not. God presented them always with the problem of faith and obedience.
>
> Solve one problem, and you will have another. This is life, and to be sick of problems is to be sick of life. Because this is God's world, every problem has its answer, and with every answer we graduate to another problem, until we finally pass on into God's eternal Kingdom and our reward.
>
> Problems are thus not only aspects of a fallen world, as well as aspects of a growing world, but they are also opportunities sent from God, to test us, to enable us to grow, and to further us in the fulfillment of our calling.[5]

Rather than respond to the Biblical calling of motherhood, many women are too willing to have their children taught and nurtured by paid substitutes. The "experts" have successfully convinced these women that their children are better off interacting with other kids under a "trained professional," learning arts and crafts in school-type settings from the time they are barely walking. These children don't learn how to be part of a family, but rather how to be part of a col-

---

5   R. J. Rushdoony, *A Word in Season*, Vol. 1 (Vallecito, CA: Ross House Books, 2010), 138–9.

lective in group settings where the caretakers often have little more investment than the paycheck they receive for keeping the children physically safe.

Are these babysitters/teachers prepared to love the child enough to deal with his selfish spirit? Are they prepared to fully deal with deceit when it makes its appearance? Or, do they just "make peace" and convince the child that she can have or do whatever she wants, whenever she wants, just so long as there is an appearance of coopera-tion (John 10:12–13)?

If we train our children in this fashion, they will grow up to look to the "village" to make up for their shortcomings, bail them out of bad investments, and excuse their bad behavior, often shifting the blame onto their parents. (I would agree that the parents are the guilty par-ty as charged, but not because they were "mean" to their children. Rather, it is because they indulged their children instead of discipling them.) Rather than develop into culture-changers, Christian children raised in this fashion become part of the culture that needs to be changed.

A portion of dialogue near the conclusion of the 1962 film *The Miracle Worker*[6] involves Helen Keller's father thanking her tutor, An-nie Sullivan, after she succeeded in improving Helen's behavior and obedience. I share it here to make an important point:

> CAPTAIN KELLER: Miss Annie, your first month's salary. With many more to come, I trust. It doesn't pay our debt for what you've done.
>
> ANNIE SULLIVAN: I've taught her one thing: No. Don't do this, don't do that.
>
> CAPTAIN KELLER: It's more than we could do.
>
> ANNIE SULLIVAN: I wanted to teach her what language is. I know that without it, to do nothing but obey is no gift. Obedience without understanding is blindness, too. I don't know what else to do. I simply go on and keep doing what

---

6   I recommend any mother who is struggling with affecting a change of attitude and behavior with her children to watch this film. The scene in the kitchen as teacher and student battle for which one will be in control inspires me each and every time I watch it.

I've done and have faith that inside she's waiting, like water underground. You can help, Captain Keller.

CAPTAIN KELLER: How?

ANNIE SULLIVAN: The world is not an easy place for anyone. I don't want her just to obey. But to let her have her way in everything is a lie—to her. You've got to stand between that lie and her.

And that is what God has called mothers to do—to stand between the lies of the flesh, the world, and devil—and relentlessly teach their children while their hearts are still tender. Mothers who teach their children what sin is help them identify it in their lives. By refusing to shield them from the consequences of disobedience, they are planting the seeds for culture-changing growth. The results of the opposite worldview in practice are all around us.

CONCLUSION

Otto Scott's insight bears repeating: *God is no buttercup.* Doug Wilson comments:

> Otto Scott put it well when he said that the God of the Bible is no buttercup. And when Jesus came He revealed all the attributes of the Father, and not just those things which we can easily interpret as comforting to ourselves. But the Lord's words were simultaneously blunt and pointed, and as Chesterton put it, "He did not hesitate to throw furniture down the front steps of the Temple." However, we like to hear all about love, and mercy, and comfort, and kindness. This is not bad in itself; these are all biblical revelations of God's nature and character. But we present them out of context; we neglect the wrath, and holiness, and justice of God. We do not neglect these attributes because they are contradictions to the first set; we neglect them because we do not know how the Bible reconciles them.

Notice how the apostle seats them at the table together, as though they were good friends. "Therefore consider the goodness and severity of God: on those who fell, severity; but toward you, goodness, if you continue in His goodness" (Rom. 11:22). We must constantly remember that a half-truth presented as the whole truth is an untruth. God is kind, and God is severe. Jesus reveals the nature of the Father to us; Jesus is kind, and Jesus is severe.[7]

Proverbs 6:20–23 states that parents are the responsible parties when it comes to inculcating a worldview that identifies God's commandments as the lamp and light which will lead, protect, inform, and reprove children as they move through life.

The God of the Bible is holy and calls us to be holy as He is holy (Lev. 20:26 and 1 Peter 1:16). The problem with too many who claim Christ as their Lord and Savior is aptly exposited in the lyrics of the song "Be Like Him!":

> You know a lot of people have their own ideas of what
>   God is like and how we should live.
> But our authority is God's word alone,
> If we want to know what to believe.
> You see, you thought God was just like you, willing to
>   wink at sin, but He
> tells us plainly in His word that we must *be like Him*.[8]

---

7 http://www.dougwils.com/Old-Table-Talk-Articles/What-Would-Jesus-Damn.html, accessed 6-12-12

8 http://judylyrics.klsoaps.com/WW.html, from the CD "Walkin' Wise" by Judy Rogers.

2

You Have Heard It Said

*P*eople, whether they like it or acknowledge it, are products of their culture. We all are born into an ongoing story and absorb premises and presuppositions from early on in our lives. Many who profess belief and loyalty to Jesus Christ and His Holy Word have been educated by those outside the faith and hold a multitude of conclusions drawn from faulty premises. Even within the ranks of Christian homeschooling, too few parents re-examine views they've held since childhood, and fail to use a Biblical lens to evaluate whether cultural norms are in fact Biblical norms.

Take, for example, the concept of "sharing." How many children are forced to allow other children to run roughshod over their belongings because their parents have told them they "have" to share? Is this "rule" a Biblical one, or does it stem from socialistic propaganda that advocates the redistribution of property and capital?

Even in Jesus' day, the religious leaders had perverted God's law to the point that Jesus rebuked them:

> *Woe unto you, scribes and Pharisees, hypocrites! For ye compass sea and land to make one proselyte, and when he is made, ye make him twofold more the child of hell than yourselves. (Matt. 23:15)*

Jesus would begin many of His teachings with the phrase, "You have heard it said," and then follow up with, "But I say." In each case, He was addressing some aspect of the Mosaic law that had been hijacked by the religious leaders of His day for their own purposes. As a result, their disciples were unwittingly offending God while under the impression that they were being righteous.

The voice of the modern church is one of accommodation rather than godly rebuke. The "pluralistic" mindset that has been continually force-fed leaves most who enter congregations feeling that all they need is minor tweaking in their lives rather than a complete overhaul. We've been told so often and for so long not to "judge," that "acceptance" has become the mark of holiness, rather than calling people to repentance. As a result, scooping necklines, drooping trousers, body piercings, and the like are all acceptable so long as there are vocal professions of faith to override them.

So, how is anyone to discern if his presuppositions and resultant actions are in line with a Biblical worldview? The answer lies in knowing the law of God within the context of redemption and how it constitutes a faith for all of life. Ecclesiastes concludes,

> *Let us hear the conclusion of the whole matter: Fear God, and keep his commandments: for this is the whole duty of man. For God shall bring every work into judgment, with every secret thing, whether it be good, or whether it be evil.* (Eccles. 12:13–14)

Thus, by examining the "givens" in life within the framework of God's law-word, a believer will stand on surer footing when it comes to living out the faith in all spheres and arenas of life. God's law separates the fact from fiction.

LITTLE KNOWN FACTS

The musical comedy *You're a Good Man, Charlie Brown* features a song sung by the know-it-all Lucy entitled "Little Known Facts."[1]

---

1 Music and lyrics by Clark Gesner based on the characters created by cartoonist Charles M. Schulz.

Do you see that tree? / It is a Fir tree. / It's called a Fir tree because it gives us fur, / For coats. / It also gives us wool in the wintertime.

This is an elm tree. / It's very little. / But it will grow up into a giant tree, / An oak. / You can tell how old it is by counting its leaves…

And way up there, / Those fluffy little white things, / Those are clouds; / They make the wind blow. / And way down there, / Those tiny little black things, / Those are bugs. / They make the grass grow…

And this thing here, / It's called a hydrant. / They grow all over, / And no one seems to know / Just how / A little thing like that / Gives so much water.

D'you see that bird? / It's called an Eagle, / But since it's little it has another name, / A Sparrow. / And on Christmas and Thanksgiving / We eat them.

And way up there, / The little stars and planets, / Make the rain, / That falls in showers. / And when it's cold and winter is upon us, / The snow comes up, / Just like the flowers.

After it comes up, the wind blows it around so it / Looks like it's coming down but actually it comes up / Out of the ground—like grass. It comes up, Charlie Brown, / Snow comes up!

It is easy to laugh at these ridiculous explanations, but how many similar "explanations" have millions of students (and people in general) been fed and swallowed since their youth, not only in humanistic schools but in churches, too, simply because someone in a position of authority proclaimed them as true? Some examples:

- The earth is billions of years old, and all life began as a result of a Big Bang.

- The fetus is not a person.
- A family is defined by people living together who love each other.

But there are other, more subtle deceptions that many believers buy into that result in long-term negative consequences for themselves and their families.

Take, for example, the Pledge of Allegiance, which reads:

I pledge allegiance to the Flag
Of the United States of America,
And to the Republic for which it stands:
One Nation under God, indivisible,
With Liberty and Justice for all.

How many have ever questioned the origins and premises of this oath?

Most Americans believe that the Pledge of Allegiance to the flag was the work of the eighteenth-century founding fathers. In fact, the Pledge did not come about until 1892. It was authored by Francis Bellamy, a defrocked Baptist minister from Boston who identified himself as a "Christian Socialist" and was removed from the pulpit for preaching politics, specifically for espousing the view that "Jesus was a socialist."[2]

Although not in the original form, the phrase "under God" was added in 1954 and has somehow legitimized this "loyalty oath" to many professing believers. Because they have compartmentalized their Christian faith and divorced it from politics and history, they miss the fact that the pledge has "much less to do with expressing love for one's country, than more or less blind obedience to the consolidated, centralized state that was created in the aftermath of the War between the States."[3]

Most Christians think that the solution to our problems is to vote conservative, and many show more loyalty to America than to Christ. They fail to see that God's law-word is a seamless garment and not

---

2   Thomas J. DiLorenzo, *Lincoln Unmasked: What You're Not Supposed to Know About Dishonest Abe* (New York: Three Rivers Press, 2006), 156.
3   Ibid., 19.

a patchwork quilt of unrelated commandments. Jesus summarized the law in two great commandments. The Ten Commandments are an expansion of the two, with the case law designed to demonstrate practical applications. Thus, when you break one of God's commandments, you really break all because of that unity. Rushdoony points out,

> [W]hile a man's faith has immediate consequences, those consequences are not necessarily apparent at once. Thus, a man who builds without a foundation has at once endangered his life's structure, but that collapse will become apparent only with a storm. People who try to establish their lives and their children's lives on a character without faith, on morality without roots, have thereby destroyed their future. The fact that the damage may only become apparent years later does not nullify the causal relationship.[4]

Just as general computer viruses don't damage immediately, but hide alongside other programs, false premises or revisionist information piggybacked on well-established facts spread in a viral manner throughout our thoughts and life. Just as trojan viruses masquerade as something they're not and eventually damage or erase a hard disk, so too the unquestioned or unexamined acceptance of what is taught will take its toll in a comprehensive way in our lives and the lives of future generations. It is only through a systematic study of the full counsel of God that one can identify the many "viruses" that have made their way into a person's computations.

Uncovering these infections would be an insurmountable task were it not for the reality that:

> *All Scripture is given by inspiration of God, and is profitable for doctrine, for reproof, for correction, for instruction in righteousness: That the man of God may be perfect, thoroughly furnished unto all good works.* (2 Tim. 3:16-17)

---

4   R. J. Rushdoony, *The Institutes of Biblical Law, Vol. 2: Law and Society* (Vallecito, CA: Ross House Books, 1982), 532.

In order to be thoroughly furnished unto all good works, nothing should be taken at face value without examining it first through the lens of Scripture.

> [T]he man who hears the Lord's words and obeys them is the man who lives in terms of God's reality. Consequences are real to him, because actions are not autonomous nor isolated. All thoughts, acts, and words occur in God's universe, and all have their consequences in terms of the world of God's law. Nothing exists in autonomy or isolation from God and His law word. Every moment, thought, and event is inextricably linked to God's total word and is inseparable from it. To be godly means in part recognizing that we are creatures of God, His creation and for His purpose and glory, and in seeing our lives in their totality as a part of that purpose. Then, instead of piecemeal religion, we have a Biblical faith.[5]

In My Life

Back in the seventies as a newly married couple, my husband and I didn't have many possessions. What we had came as a result of gifts from family and weekend garage sales where we snatched up bargains. We were regularly counseled by friends that we should acquire credit cards, run up some bills, pay them off, and thereby establish a good credit rating. This, we were told, was how to become established, and someday we'd be able to buy a home. I remember the feeling of power when I saw something I wanted and could charge it. I even took enormous pleasure when I paid the monthly bills, knowing that I was on my way to becoming a good credit risk.

We were nine years into our marriage when a friend introduced us to the writings of R. J. Rushdoony, specifically his *Institutes of Biblical Law*. My husband and I were so taken with the book that we began to

---

5   Ibid., 533.

fight over who was going to get to read it.[6] Slowly but surely, we were developing a Biblical mindset, something that we had longed for but up until that point had never acquired. There were many instances where we concluded that premises and perspectives that we'd been taught or picked up were simply not true. We began to reorder our lives so that every area was examined from a Biblical perspective. One episode sticks out in my mind, when an established way of living was confronted with the truth of God's Word faithfully expounded.

We returned home one evening after a long day of shopping in Carmel, California. The whole family was glowing over our purchases, and my husband led us in a prayer of thanksgiving after we examined how much we had been able to buy. After dinner, I sat down to read some Rushdoony, specifically his little gem *Law & Liberty*. Within an hour, I told my husband that we had thanked the wrong person. We shouldn't have thanked God for our purchases of the day; we should have thanked MasterCard. I read to him:

> [P]rivate property and moral order are closely linked together. When men are governed by God, they are more provident, more inclined to be debt-free, more responsible in their management of their families and affairs, and much more prone to own, cherish and husband property wisely. A high incidence of debt-free property indicates a high degree of godly living which is both provident and free of covetousness, for it is covetousness which breeds debt-living. The basic principle of Scripture is clear-cut: "Owe no man anything, but to love one another" (Rom. 13:8). We do not truly own property unless it is debt-free. Debt is in essence a form of slavery, and the basic function of private property is to establish us in material liberty. A man who covets property of various kinds but cannot live debt-free is not seeking property on godly terms but on covetous terms.[7]

6　The solution was easy: I read Volume 1, and he began with Volume 2.

7　Rushdoony, *Law & Liberty* (Vallecito, CA: Ross House Books, 1984, 2009), 85.

That night we took inventory of our financial situation. Ten years into our marriage, we had two children, two car payments, and almost $15,000 in unsecured debt. With paying the interest on this balance, it dawned on me that we were paying interest for meals that had been eaten, digested, and eliminated. Also, any "great bargains" we procured while purchasing on credit, ended up costing us more than the original price tag. It was then that we had to confront the sinful premises and perspectives in which we were abiding. Dr. Rushdoony's words stung but were redemptive.

> In Colossians 3:5, St. Paul defines evil covetousness as idolatry, and he declares that it is a sin that we must mortify or destroy in ourselves. Such covetousness seeks to exalt the man and to increase his possessions, but because it grounds itself on sin rather than God's law, it is destructive of both man and property. Those who move in terms of God's word become the blessed meek, the tamed of God, of whom the Psalmist says, *"The meek shall inherit the earth; and shall delight themselves in the abundance of peace"* (Ps. 37:11).[8]

After this, we increased the earnestness with which we studied God's law and worked our way out of debt. Corrections were made in our thinking, resulting in some drastic changes in our lifestyle.

Another instance comes to mind where, instead of having to alter our course of action, we discovered that by God's grace we had embarked on a path that was surprisingly orthodox.

During one of our first in-person meetings with Dr. Rushdoony (after having read a number of his books), he inquired about where my son was being educated. Not knowing that the man who stood in front of me in my living room was considered the father of the modern Christian school and homeschooling movements, I sheepishly answered, "Actually, we homeschool." He gave a resounding, "Excellent!" and proceeded to fill my arms with his books on education and a number written by Sam Blumenfeld. I commented to my husband later on, "Guess what? We're accidentally doing the right thing!" How-

---

8   Ibid.

ever, in retrospect, there was nothing accidental about God's loving, providential hand directing us. The Scriptures are clear that those who ask, receive; those who seek, find; and those who knock will find an opened door (Matt. 7:7-11).

As I continued to read Rushdoony's works, my commitment solidified to provide my children with an education that was not piecemeal, but systematic and thoroughly Biblical. Our family learned that there was nothing piecemeal about living out the implications of God's Word.

> Modern man seems to believe in piecemeal religion: he thinks it is possible to profess Biblical faith on the Lord's Day, repeating the Apostle's Creed. On Monday, he sends his children to a state school which teaches humanism. He works in terms of non-biblical economics in a humanistic state. And he sees no contradiction. Our Lord however, was emphatic: piecemeal religion is an impossibility: "No man can serve two masters: for either he will hate the one, and love the other; or else he will hold to the one, and despise the other. Ye cannot serve God and mammon" (Matt. 6:24).[9]

THE CONCLUSION OF THE MATTER

Only when all areas of life and thought are examined within the context of Scripture will we be able to discern between truth and falsehoods and unearth errors in our thinking. This examination needs to be systematic if we are going to advance the Kingdom of God on His terms.

The Bible, it cannot be repeated often enough, was not given to man to be an inspiring word, but the command word. It is not intended to please man, but to declare to him what he is in himself, and what he must be in the Lord. The Bible is inspired, not inspiring; it is infallible, because it is the word of God.

---

9   Rushdoony, *Law and Society*, 527.

A systematic Biblical theology will thus find it impossible to limit the religious realm to the ecclesiastical domain. God is totally God and Lord: the universe is totally under Him and His law-word. A systematic theology which is faithful to the living God will thus speak to the totality of man and his life.[10]

Proverbs 3:7 instructs us: *"Be not wise in thine own eyes: fear the* LORD, *and depart from evil."* That is how we discern between the "You have heard it said" fallacies and the truth of what God's Word declares. Jesus promised in John 16:12–15 that the Holy Spirit would guide us in all truth and take what is Christ's and impart it to us. Systematically following the Lord's commands with humility and gratitude is the path to victory.

---

10   Rushdoony, *Systematic Theology* (Vallecito, CA: Ross House Books, 1994), 117.

3

The Mediatorial Work of the Law

*C*halcedon has long chronicled the sins against the family by the church and the state. Identifying the causes and consequences of these attacks helps God's people see the effects of them in their families' lives. However, there are Scriptures directly relating to the family that are ignored or disregarded as though they have passed away. These transgressions are categorized as abominations by God. Christian families must rectify this ignorance, so that God's blessings may again flow into our families and culture. It is hard to conceive of God blessing any endeavor to restore "family values" when His values have been categorically dismissed.

In determining how the family is to live and serve the Kingdom of God, examine the personal relationships within the family to ascertain whether or not the family is adhering to the call to "the righteousness of the law" (Rom 8:4). Rushdoony explains,

> *No direct relationship is possible between persons except through the law of God.* Attempts to by-pass the law for a person-to-person confrontation without God means the judgment of God, for the law is operative against its violators and against the destruction of the true relationship of man to man under God's law.[1]

---

1   R. J. Rushdoony, *Institutes of Biblical Law*, *Vol. 1* (Phillipsburg, NJ: Presbyterian and Reformed Publishing Co., 1973), 431.

Here Rushdoony makes an important distinction to avoid the charge of salvation by law:

> To speak of the mediatorial work of the law is to arouse immediately the hostility of Protestant evangelicals, with their deeply rooted antinomianism. To clarify the matter as quickly as possible, Jesus Christ is the only mediator between God and Man. There is no salvation except through Jesus Christ, the God-given mediator and redeemer. The mediation of Jesus Christ is *between God and man*; the law is the God-given mediator *between man and man*.[2]

By understanding and living out the implications of God's ordained relationships within the family, the ability to influence church, school, vocations, free associations, and the civil government will be established on a surer footing.

HUSBAND AND WIFE

Rushdoony points out that although marriage is the most intimate of all earthly relationships, it remains a mediated one circumscribed by specific laws:

> The law of the Lord concerning sexual relations during menstruation is a clear illustration of this principle. It is impossible for man to claim that within marriage a non-theological person-to-person confrontation is possible. The relationship is one which is entirely circumscribed by law. It is ordained by God and therefore governed by His law … The law extends to … forbidding relations with a menstruous wife or with a wife not fully recovered from childbirth.[3]

---

2   Ibid.
3   Ibid., 431–432.

Those outside the faith often ridicule this law, dismissing relations during these times as areas of personal preference. Many Christian married couples would assert that although they have no wish to participate in sexual relations during menstruation, God doesn't really care when they have sex. They have created a God-free zone. Yet, the Bible calls for deliberate violators of this law to be "cut off from among their people" (Lev. 20:18).[4] These are strong words, and there is little justification to assume that God's opinions have changed. Violations of these restrictions lead to "a sickened land" and a "revolted nature" and move the earth itself to spue out a people (Lev. 20:22).[5]

Is it safe to assume that these are merely historical conventions, when Ezekiel includes those who follow them as among the righteous?

> 5.   But if a man be just, and do that which is lawful and right,
> 6.   And hath not eaten upon the mountains, neither hath lifted up his eyes to the idols of the house of Israel, neither hath defiled his neighbour's wife, neither hath come near to a menstruous woman …
> 9.   Hath walked in my statutes, and hath kept my judgments, to deal truly; he is just, he shall surely live, saith the Lord GOD. (Ezek. 18:5–6, 9; emphasis added)

The Scriptures also discuss in detail a period of abstinence from sexual intercourse between a husband and wife after the birth of a child. Leviticus 12:2–5 reads:

> 2.   If a woman have conceived seed, and born a man child: then she shall be unclean seven days; according to the days of the separation for her infirmity shall she be unclean.
> 3.   And in the eighth day the flesh of his foreskin shall be circumcised.

---

4   Quoted from John Peter Lange, *Commentary on the Holy Scriptures: Leviticus* (Grand Rapids: Zondervan), 155, in Rushdoony, *Institutes, Vol. 1*, 427.
5   The reader is encouraged to read Rushdoony's treatment of this and related subject matter in the section covering the Seventh Commandment in *Institutes*.

4. And she shall then continue in the blood of her pu-
    rifying three and thirty days; she shall touch no hal-
    lowed thing, nor come into the sanctuary, until the
    days of her purifying be fulfilled.
5. But if she bear a maid child, then she shall be un-
    clean two weeks, as in her separation: and she shall
    continue in the blood of her purifying threescore and
    six days.

Rushdoony notes,

> Twice the time for purification is required for a woman
> after giving birth to a girl as to a boy. Here as in other laws
> there are physiological aspects as well as ecclesiastical
> ones. The fact that we are ignorant of these as yet should
> give us the humility to reserve judgment and to accept the
> fact, hard as it is for the human mind to accept, that God
> is wiser than we are. In Paul's words, "Because the foolish-
> ness of God is wiser than men; and the weakness of God
> is stronger than men" (1 Cor. 1:25).[6]

If we begin with the premise that God is wise and just, even when
we cannot understand Him, we may do badly in the sight of men, but
we will be blessed by God.

I doubt that much premarital counsel includes discussion of these
prohibitions, though it should. Along with providing a health protec-
tion for women, these laws establish that domination is not to be a
part of the marital relationship, as God has given limits and bounds
to sexual activity even within heterosexual monogamy. While we may
not know or ever fully understand the reasons behind some of these
laws, they are indisputably significant to God.

---

6   Rushdoony, *Leviticus* (Vallecito, CA: Ross House Books), 130.

SUBMISSION

It should be noted that within the context of godly submission of the wife to her husband, God has not placed her in a role of servitude but as partner. Ephesians 5:24 is commonly interpreted to mean a total subjection of women to their husbands as of the church to Christ. Rushdoony answers, "This would be a justifiable claim only if husbands were as perfect and sinless as Christ."[7]

While God ordains a prescribed chain of command within the family, He never permits one human being to dominate another. Thus what is true regarding sexual access also pertains to other aspects of the marital relationship. Men who assert that their wives are to submit without comment or question are demanding a totalitarian obedience. This negates the fundamental premise that authority in all spheres of life and at all times is limited by the prior authority of God.[8]

Nowhere in the Bible do you see any directive for men to treat their wives as doormats. Sarah, even in her rebuke of her husband (Gen. 16), was backed up by God and subsequently commended as an example for her godliness and submission (1 Pet. 3:6).

The authority of God is absolute; the authority of man is always conditional.[9]

PARENT AND CHILD

Just as there can be no unmediated relationship between husband and wife, so too, the parent/child relationship is one that is circumscribed by God's law-word. By failing to appreciate the extent to which Scripture defines this relationship, many embark on this aspect of family life without a map or compass.

The family is the first school, church, and social environment for children. God's Word needs to be the foundation for training and discipline. The blessing of children is not in what they do for parents,

---

7   Rushdoony, *Salvation and Godly Rule* (Vallecito, CA: Ross House Books), 494.
8   Ibid., 495.
9   Ibid.

but in the opportunity for parents to exercise godly stewardship in their children's lives. Too many parents treat this "blessing" more like a trophy. Rather than making a thoroughly Biblical education a top priority, they spend lavish time and resources on sports and leisure activities at the expense of godly character training. Most leave their children's education in the hands of the state school with its atheistic orientation, and think that a weekly vaccination of Sunday school is all that is needed to instill a Christian worldview. Subsequently, when their children act out the logical consequences of such evolutionary based education and become criminal (whether apprehended or not), parents whine and moan but often bail them out of trouble. The Scriptures strongly address this issue:

18. If a man have a stubborn and rebellious son, which will not obey the voice of his father, or the voice of his mother, and that, when they have chastened him, will not hearken unto them:
19. Then shall his father and his mother lay hold on him, and bring him out unto the elders of his city, and unto the gate of his place;
20. And they shall say unto the elders of his city, This our son is stubborn and rebellious, he will not obey our voice; he is a glutton, and a drunkard.
21. And all the men of his city shall stone him with stones, that he die: so shalt thou put evil away from among you; and all Israel shall hear, and fear. (Deut. 21:18–21)

The incorrigible person is an adult who refuses to obey authority and receive correction. In today's world this penalty seems overly harsh, but in truth, when our country rooted its laws in Christian principles, this used to be the regular practice. This law, if followed, eliminates a criminal class from society.

How many jails are full of repeat offenders because the evil not only remains unpurged, but is subsidized? Rushdoony notes,

This law, however, is not only about habitual criminals; it is also about the family. *Not blood but faith must be the determining factor.* The family, having the fullest knowledge, under normal circumstances, of a son's criminality, has the moral obligation to report him to the authorities...

Those who hate this text insist on calling the *son* a child, or a baby, and on accusing Scripture of demanding that little children be executed. The text is clear that the son is an adult who is in total war against society in word, thought, and deed. He resists radically any attempt by the family to control him.

The parents have the duty to take the lead in the son's arrest and prosecution. A choice is required of them. The son may be living elsewhere, but their status as parents requires them to choose God's justice against the family's solidarity. If the family, God's basic institution, does not favor justice over blood, neither church nor state is likely to be strong.

This means that *lesser* steps must have preceded this radical step. The parents had the duty, where and when possible, earlier, to rebuke and chastise their child. In some instances, it could mean requiring the son to leave the family's home if the rebelliousness continued. The law simply summarizes all this. In following these steps, the parents make it clear that their loyalty is to God's future, not to a wayward family member.[10]

Rather than the socialistic perspective that it takes a village to raise a child, the Bible states that the family is to raise the children. As parents and extended family assume the responsibility of teaching, correcting, and disciplining their members, they bolster the institution of the family and qualify for generational blessings. Bringing a rebellious son to the city gate is the God-ordained prescription of putting the evil away from us.

What legacy do we leave to future generations when we have not modeled righteousness to them? In a very real sense, the blessing involved with being a parent is to represent God to one's children and

---

10   Rushdoony, *Deuteronomy* (Vallecito, CA: Ross House Books), 318.

demonstrate that love, by placing loyalty to His royal law over and above biological ties.

Gender Distinctions

Today's mindset demands apologies when boys and girls are intentionally treated differently. But to treat male and female children differently is to honor the God who "created them male and female" with differing roles and jurisdictions. To obscure the distinctions is something that all humanistic and statist societies work relentlessly to achieve.

A significant law appears in Deuteronomy 22:5, which points out the strong repulsion God has for mixing gender roles,

> *The woman shall not wear that which pertaineth unto a man, neither shall a man put on a woman's garment: for all that do so are abomination unto the* Lord *thy God.*

This prohibition against transvestitism is not simply a law about fashion or style of clothing; it has a much broader meaning and implication. It applies to the standards and practices for gender roles within the family. How parents deal with their sons and expect their sons to deal with their sisters sets the standards for society in general.

> The law, therefore, forbids imposing a man's duties and tools on a woman, and a woman's on a man. Its purpose is thus to maintain the fundamental order. A man who allows his wife to support him when he is able-bodied has violated this law.[11]

This means that rather than promote a false "equality," family life should consist of mothers modeling for their daughters what a Proverbs 31 woman does, while fathers guide their sons toward the dual roles of protector and provider. Brothers and sisters should relate to

---

11   Rushdoony, *Institutes of Biblical Law, Vol. 1*, 435–436.

each other acknowledging the physical, emotional, and positional roles God ordains for each, in preparation for every other relationship they will encounter.

Instead of Biblical patterns of gender distinction, today we see the feminization of men and the masculinization of women. This breeds chaos and disorder and undermines the institution of the family. Rushdoony points out,

> The purpose of the law is to increase the strength and authority of men and women in their respective domains. The strength of men is in being men under God, and the strength of women is in being women under God.
>
> The definition of transvestite thus must be made broader than a mere reference to clothing.
>
> It can be added that modern culture has a strongly transvestite character. Here as elsewhere, it prefers the character of perversion to the law of God.[12]

In our day we see women in law enforcement roles, theaters of war, and eldership in the church. The working mom is deemed to have chosen the nobler route in pursuing ecclesiastical or civil service, often leaving children in the care of paid caregivers. God's Word describes such practices as abominations, and although He doesn't outline the punishment for these transgressions, He does exact societal penalty. If men do not respect God's order as laid out In the beginning, God will exact justice in ways that get our attention.

CONCLUSION

God is the same yesterday, today, and forever. Practices that were identified as abominations in the books of Moses or by the prophets are not transformed into neutral areas or issues of no concern to God.

---

12   Ibid., 437–438.

The family as trustee is responsible before God to know His law, teach it, and oversee the obedience to it.

Before the family can reverse its course, and that of society, it must have a Biblical law-faith rather than a humanistic and atomistic one. The family must again become the trustee of God's covenantal requirements, and a trustee under God of children and property.[13]

---

13   Ibid., 418.

4

Take Your Time:
Step Knowledgeably into Marriage

*L*ove at first sight may seem to work out perfectly in novels and film, but rarely are first impressions true or lasting. Along with this myth comes the illusion that family background, religious orientation, and lifetime experiences are of little-to-no importance when it comes to committing to lifelong marriage. Young people smitten by the love bug believe the age-old lies that *love will keep them together* and that *love is all they need*. However, doing things God's way remains the touchstone for successful covenant marriage.

The Bible provides definite guidelines for entering into the most intimate of all human relationships. Among them are: chastity before marriage; the dowry presented to the girl's father demonstrating the husband's ability and willingness to provide for the new family; exemption from military service for the man for a year's time; specific times and circumstances when the couple is to refrain from marital intimacy; and specific consequences for offenses within the marriage. In addition, the education for the children, residential proximity to family, along with perspectives on nutrition, finances, medical care, indebtedness, etc., will play into the success or failure of the marriage.

I wonder how many couples are counseled to explore all of these and other matters before deciding to marry? More time is spent on selecting invitations and a venue for the reception. The wedding receives a lot of attention, much more so than the ensuing marriage.

Most marriage vows include the phrasing, *for better for worse, for richer for poorer, in sickness and in health, until death do us part*. Too few really fathom what this could entail. While young couples are newly smitten and head over heels in love with each other, they and their counselors downplay how bad things can become in their relationship. But the loss of one's job, one's health, the illness or death of a child, or even the loss of the spark of romance are rarely, if ever, considered ahead of time. The rising divorce rate, even among professing Christians, speaks to this fact.

Some argue that it is impossible to prepare for all contingencies at the outset of a marriage. While the particulars can't be known ahead of time, the manner in which circumstances will be dealt certainly can. Will God's law be the standard for making decisions, or will personal convenience and preferences rule the day? Will a mutual respect be maintained for each other's family so that both spouses are willing to receive counsel from family members when problems arise?

My father often spoke of the counseling he and my mother had prior to their marriage when he would explain decisions that were made in our family. How we were educated, where we lived, the sort of medical practice he would have—all were matters of faith to him, and all were discussed with the family. He took his responsibilities to my mother seriously, so much so that when she became an invalid after a series of strokes, he converted our living room into her room and she remained at home rather than take many family members' advice to put her in a managed care facility. Growing up, there were times I resented this intrusion into normal living. But as an adult, I see that he took his commitment to her seriously—that he would be her provider and caretaker *for worse, for poorer, in sickness, until death parted them.* Years later he remarried, and again his commitment was tested when his second wife suffered a stroke. He continued to care for her for thirteen years until he was almost 90 and no longer able to provide suitable care because of his own health issues.

Marriage is not just a contract/covenant between two people; it includes their families as well. This is apparent when nasty divorce proceedings demonstrate how the extended family is often adversely affected by the choice of a husband or wife, not to mention the impact on the children.

Parents should teach their children the realities of marriage by example and instruction. Family members being involved in the earliest stages of any courtship will bolster the chances that good counsel can follow in the case of disagreements. A courtship should be long enough so that there are opportunities for conflict and Biblical resolution to arise, as well as the behavior of the man and woman examined and discussed. Rather than fall in love, the couple can step into marriage knowledgeably.

R. J. Rushdoony prayed eloquently after a teaching on the Doctrine of Marriage:

> OUR LORD AND OUR GOD, we thank Thee that Thou hast established and ordained marriage for the welfare and happiness of mankind. We thank Thee that Thou hast called us into Christian marriages, made us husbands and fathers, wives and mothers in Jesus Christ. Bless each home that is here represented that by Thy grace we may grow and mature in terms of our calling, rejoice in one another in Thee and under Thee, and might all the days of our life know the joy and the strength that comes from being heirs together of the grace of life. Bless us to this purpose, in Jesus' name. Amen.[1]

---

1   Elizabeth Fellerson, ed., *Towards a Christian Marriage* (Vallecito, CA: Ross House/ Chalcedon), 17.

5

The Expectation for Children

$\mathcal{I}$t is painful to witness a young child ordering his parents around. The only thing more painful is to witness the child's parents (many times professing Christians) awkwardly smile and give in to the child's demand. Sometimes you can hear parents negotiate with the child, attempting to get him to "speak politely" to them. I recall my children's faces when they would see this dynamic played out. They would appear conflicted, as though they wished they had such freedom to rule our household. They would, however, inevitably announce later, "That child really needed a spanking." I would point out to them that they were correct in their assessment that the boy or girl really needed disciplining, but I would add, "Truth be told, the parents need a spanking!"

My children were taught that if a parent failed to discipline a child, that child had a parent who hated him because the Bible teaches: "He who spares his rod hates his son, But he who loves him disciplines him promptly" (Prov. 13:24 NKJV).

Why do modern parents tolerate the tantrums, rudeness, defiance, and rebellion of their children? Why do they pursue a policy of appeasement, often handling a defiant outburst with a piece of candy or a new toy? Blame can be laid at the doorstep of the anti-spanking experts who have polluted the culture by making corporal punishment synonymous with child abuse, thereby creating justifiable fear in parents that public disciplining may get them in trouble with the law or Child Protective Services. While there are a number of societal causes that contribute to the status quo, much needs to be laid at the doorsteps of the church that fails to teach God's law-word in its fullest application.

The Word of God warns us that foolishness is bound up in the hearts of children (Prov. 22:15), and children who fail to honor their God-given authority will reap the consequences of an undisciplined life (Deut. 5:16). Parents who ignore the Bible's instructions to identify, reprove, and correct rebellion and defiance in their children bear responsibility for the actions and outcomes of those children even into adulthood. Those parents who are not self-consciously submitted to the authority of God, who operate without a Biblical understanding of the family, and who approach parenthood as a make-up-the-rules-as-you-go activity, scandalize their children by being unfaithful representatives.[1] With all the excellent resources available to instruct how to discipline Biblically, parents are doubly without excuse.

The Root of the Problem

A warped understanding of the purpose of marriage contributes to our modern parenting failures. Sadly, many decide to marry without a Biblical understanding that the family is God's basic institution of society and that God's plan for discipling the nations begins with the fruit of the womb. Couples and their parents often give more attention to the color scheme at the wedding and the favors the guests will receive, than what the Bible says about the creation of a new Christian family. They approach their marriage with the assumption that it will evolve and progress naturally without much direct instruction from the Word.

In Genesis 1:28, God instructs Adam and Eve to be fruitful and multiply—in other words, to have children. Many enter marriage with something other than this dominion mandate in mind and have elevated other priorities ahead of bringing children into the world: finishing school, establishing themselves in a career, buying a house, or traveling the world. The uncertainties of our day encourage the

---

[1]   Thanks to Rev. Mike O'Donovan of Rock of Liberty Church in Fort Worth, TX (www.rockofliberty.com) in a recent exposition of Lord's Day 39 from the Heidelberg Catechism.

decision to wait on children as does the huge debt from student loans, coupled with little or no prospect of employment.[2]

Modern culture supports these decisions to wait because, although not stated outright, there is the prevailing opinion that once children arrive on the scene, freedom and autonomy cease. This is the foundation for abortion being a woman's right. A culture of death encourages divorcing sexual intimacy from marriage and marriage from the bearing of children. If a Christian man and woman do not consider themselves ready to become parents, they should re-evaluate the purpose of getting married.

Psalm 127 reads:

1. *Except the* LORD *build the house, they labour in vain that build it: except the* LORD *keep the city, the watchman waketh but in vain.*
2. *It is vain for you to rise up early, to sit up late, to eat the bread of sorrows: for so he giveth his beloved sleep.*
3. *Lo, children are an heritage of the* LORD: *and the fruit of the womb is his reward.*
4. *As arrows are in the hand of a mighty man; so are children of the youth.*
5. *Happy is the man that hath his quiver full of them: they shall not be ashamed, but they shall speak with the enemies in the gate.* [Emphasis added.]

Why would Christian couples not want to receive God's reward and blessing of children? People only refuse gifts they don't consider valuable. God does not describe children as a financial drain. In God's economy children are deemed a blessing. The Psalmist specifies the reward as God-given. Happiness and contentment come to the man who has many children. The Psalmist describes offspring as having an important role in the defense against enemies at the gate. We should view these enemies as God's enemies and the children as

---

2 Interestingly enough, many married couples would be astonished and possibly offended to discover that their reasons for holding off on having children mirror almost exactly the reasons offered by abortion-minded women who claim that abortion is their only option due to these same considerations.

covenant soldiers advancing the work of the Kingdom in the face of opposition (v. 5).[3]

READY OR NOT?

Christian couples and their families need to re-examine what constitutes readiness for marriage. The Bible points to some necessary prerequisites: the man must be able to demonstrate his capacity to support his wife and future children, (the dowry demonstrated this),[4] the wife should be physically ready to bear children and be able to look well to the ways of her household (Ps. 128:3, Prov. 31).

In our culture, the first years of marriage have replaced the betrothal period of the past. This entire period was to complete the necessary prerequisites for marriage. Only after meeting the requirements would the couple be deemed ready to marry. Because we ignore the Biblical marital guidelines, Christian marriage is often reduced to a "legal" sexual relationship.

The Christian marriage contract has a third partner, God Almighty, who places a high premium on covenant children (Ruth 4:11).[5] A man should be established in his calling and ready to support his wife and future children, so that there are no earthly impediments to "filling his quiver." The priority is such that a man was to refrain from starting a business or serving in the military within the first year of marriage to focus on his wife and the creation of his family. Deuteronomy 24:5 states,

> *When a man hath taken a new wife, he shall not go out to war, neither shall he be charged with any business: but he*

---

3   Rev. Mike O'Donovan has an interesting view on v. 3. His take is that the reward belongs to God as much as it is given by God. So, in essence, the decision to hold off on having children is depriving God of what is lawfully His.

4   Ex. 22:16 speaks of the bride-price as normative. This is not the purchase of a woman as chattel property, but an indication of the man's commitment and ability to assume the role of husband.

5   The absence of children in a marriage is lamented by many prominent women of the Bible (e.g. Sarah, Rebecca, Rachel, and Hannah), or in some cases presented as a sign of judgment (Michal).

shall be free at home one year, and shall cheer up his wife which he hath taken.

Rushdoony points out,

> The bridegroom cannot be involved in military or civil duties. This is a requirement of very great importance because it clearly indicates the priority of the family to the nation. Religious institutions are not mentioned, because crises in such spheres are a rarity, whereas crises in national life are commonplace. No national crises can take precedence over the new marriage. Because the family is most important in God's sight, it must always be protected. The Vulgate gives an interesting reading: the groom shall "rejoice (or, take pleasure) with the wife of his youth." He is free, literally, "for his own household." He has a duty under God to establish a family as a physical and spiritual entity.[6]

In God's economy, the first year of marriage is to establish the family, recognizing that this supersedes business or national defense. This is a far cry from the perspective that eschews and postpones the arrival of children. If children are not eagerly anticipated, within the context of a Biblical framework, it is not a surprise that child rearing problems arise when the children arrive. With God's authority being dismissed, is it any wonder that parental authority is diminished?

Who Says So?

> Authority on the human scene is closely tied to status or position, but it cannot be equated with status. To illustrate, parenthood is a natural fact; giving birth to a child gives the status of a parent to the father and mother. Authority, however, is not derived from this natural fact but from God's command. "Honour thy father and thy mother:

6   R .J. Rushdoony, *Deuteronomy* (Vallecito, CA: Ross House Books, 2008), 372.

that thy days may be long upon the land which the LORD thy God giveth thee" (Ex. 20:12). This is a law from God which promises long life as a gift from God for obedience. Moreover, the commandment here is to adults to honor, not to children, who are commanded more specifically to obey (Eph. 6:1). This law has no true analogue in the world of nature.

This means that parents who seek to command their children naturalistically deny they have religious author- ity. Such mothers will tell their children of the "trauma" of conception and birth, and all their "sacrifices" for their children, and the fathers will recount how much time and money their children have cost them. The children are un- impressed: they didn't ask to be born, and none of these facts give the parents any true authority. Authority is a re- ligious fact, and unless it is religiously grounded, it quickly disappears.[7]

Back to our tyrant-in-the-making child who has no healthy fear of his parents. Every child is born with this wickedness in his heart which manifests itself as he gains new abilities. If parents do not stand on the firm foundation of God's law, they either take the path of least resistance by submitting to the child's dictates, or they can become heavy-handed and abusive.

When I informed my children that the parents who failed to cor- rect their children hated them, I had Scriptural backing: Hebrews 12:6, "For whom the Lord loveth he chasteneth, and scourgeth every son whom he receiveth." If this method of correction is good enough for God the Father, parents should not hesitate to apply such disci- pline when necessary. Furthermore, consistent application early on in a child's life has the added benefit of becoming less and less necessary as the child matures.

Today's explanations on the "bad" behaviors of children are mani- fold and have been dosed out to us by child psychologists with expres- sions/excuses such as the terrible twos, the teenage years, or boys will be boys. Charles Spurgeon does not agree.

---

7   R. J. Rushdoony, *Systematic Theology, Vol. 2* (Vallecito, CA: Ross House Books, 1994) 1140-1141.

The proverb is, "Boys will be boys," but I do not think so. They will be men, if we let them have time; unless they learn self-restraint and habits of obedience while they are boys, they are not likely to make good men. He who cannot obey is not fit to rule; he who has never learned to submit, will make a tyrant when he obtains the power. It is good that every child should be broken in, delivered from his foolish self-will, and made to feel that he has superiors, masters, and governors, and then, when it shall come to his turn to be a leader and a master he will have the more kindly fellow-feeling to those who are under him.[8]

Children pick up very early on if their parents' profession of faith matches their actions. Parents who refuse God's authority cannot lead their children to obey them or God. Irresponsible, self-indulgent adults come from somewhere; they don't just develop from out of the blue. The fabric of society, whether functional or dysfunctional, comes out of the context of family life.

TRAINING FOR GOVERNING

...[T]raining for government in church, state, and other areas is in Scripture essentially within the family. This is apparent in two key texts. *First*, in every Passover service, *beginning with the very first in Egypt*, the *instruction* and *participation* of the sons was a requirement. Every religious festival had an element of instruction in it, and it was essential in all things that the children be reared in the essentials and fundamentals of the faith. God so requires it...[Ex. 12:26–27; Ex. 13:8–14]

...The Hebrew child participated in the Passover Service. The Christian child took part in communion, for the first eight centuries everywhere, and the practice had some

---

8   The Metropolitan Tabernacle Pulpit: Sermons, Parts 249-260, by Charles Haddon Spurgeon.

prevalence still into the fourteenth century. It was clearly seen as essential that the covenant child understand the meaning of salvation and that as early as possible share the *responsibility* of the redeemed. He was taught to ask the question, because it was his responsibility to give an answer for his faith. This kind of training appears also in Joshua 4:6 where the question, "What mean ye by these stones?" requires the answer of teaching God's saving power.[9]

The question from the youngest child and resultant answer from the father is all part of the training that teaches the child that he/she has been born into a context, an already organized and ordered life. The significance of having the youngest child ask the question is so that all within the household of faith would learn, and be expected to know, the meaning behind the symbolism. To exclude children from a knowledgeable participation in the faith cripples them. How are they to understand that failing to obey will shorten their lives, if they have not been taught and then held accountable?

This theme repeats throughout the Scripture but is emphatically driven home in Psalm 78, especially verses 1–8:

1. *Give ear, O my people, to my law: incline your ears to the words of my mouth.*
2. *I will open my mouth in a parable: I will utter dark sayings of old:*
3. *Which we have heard and known, and our fathers have told us.*
4. *We will not hide them from their children, shewing to the generation to come the praises of the Lord, and his strength, and his wonderful works that he hath done.*
5. *For he established a testimony in Jacob, and appointed a law in Israel, which he commanded our fathers, that they should make them known to their children:*

---

9   R. J. Rushdoony, *Systematic Theology, Vol. 2* (Vallecito, CA: Ross House Books, 1994), 683.

6.   *That the generation to come might know them, even the children which should be born; who should arise and declare them to their children:*

7.   *That they might set their hope in God, and not forget the works of God, but keep his commandments:*

8.   *And might not be as their fathers, a stubborn and rebellious generation; a generation that set not their heart aright, and whose spirit was not stedfast with God.*

Rushdoony comments,

This whole psalm cites the lessons of history which parents must teach their children; the history lessons are illustrations of God's judgments and are to be a part of the teaching of God's law. Life must be built upon the law of God, the psalmist says, and the law must be taught to children: this is God's requirement. Without the law, and the examples of God's judgment on law-breakers in Scripture, history will be the continuing and weary round of judgment on unconfronted covenant-breakers. Even more, it is not merely knowledge of the law, but a life of faithfulness which is required. The goal is "that they might set their hope in God, and not forget the works of God, but keep his commandments" (v. 7).[10]

Biblical Expectations

Question #104 in the Heidelberg Catechism reads, *What does God require in the fifth Commandment? The answer: That I show all honor, love and faithfulness to my father and mother, and to all in authority over me; submit myself with due obedience to all their good instruction*

---

10   Ibid.

and correction, and also bear patiently with their infirmities, since it is
God's will to govern us by their hand.

> Authority begins for us in the home. God places parents
> over children. All children are to show "honor, love and
> faithfulness" to their parents. Ephesians 6:1–3 gives the
> New Testament interpretation of this commandment.
> God's promise of blessing to obedient children still stands!
> Disobedient children are wicked children who are prepar-
> ing themselves for ungodly lives and eventually hell, if they
> do not repent.[11]

Honor thy father and thy mother is the first commandment with a
promise, and must be established early on in a child's life. Otherwise
children are trapped in a sinful cycle that promises to shorten their
days and their parents become accomplices in their dire end. Con-
versely, when couples eagerly anticipate God's blessing of children
and steward these lives into obedient service, they will receive the
mercy unto thousands of them that keep the commandments of God.
This is how the Kingdom is forwarded.

---

11   Rev. Norman L. Jones, *Study Helps on The Heidelberg Catechism* (Reformed Church in
      the U.S., Publications Committee, 1981).

6

Rethinking Childbirth

$\mathcal{B}$ack in the early 1980s when the practice of homeschooling began to surface as an alternative to customary day-school options, the sentiments of many were less than favorable. Home-schooling parents were warned that they would tire of the endeavor, that their children's educational progress would be hampered, that they would grow up unable to successfully interact with others, and that success as an adult would be stifled. Decades later, thousands of homeschooled graduates have demonstrated, beyond a shadow of a doubt, that they are responsible citizens, who work to support themselves and their families, and prove to be assets wherever they serve. Rather than be at a disadvantage because of being homeschooled, many educated in this manner often demonstrate an "unfair" advantage. Excellent results changed the minds of critics and struck a blow to the "expert" mentality that got its start with Dr. Benjamin Spock, who convinced parents that they needed to be guided by people who were highly trained and knew more than they did.

Thanks to the foundational thesis supplied by R. J. Rushdoony,[1] large numbers of Christian families removed or never placed their children in state schools and thus recaptured an important area of family life. The pioneers of the modern movement acted on faith, believing that if they applied the Bible's directives to teach children to love God and keep His commandments, they would be blessed. Today, homeschooling has become an accepted practice, although

---

[1] Rushdoony was among those who demonstrated that homeschooling was far from a new practice and that through most of the history of the U.S. republic and during the colonial period, parents teaching their children was common-place and the literacy rate in America was much higher than today.

efforts to stifle and regulate it still persist. Thanks to many faithful homeschooling advocacy groups that combat legislative efforts to steal from the family that which God commanded it to do, homeschooling continues to be a growing movement.

Education, however, is *not* the only area where Biblical considerations have been usurped by so-called "experts." Like education, modern medical childbirth procedures, along with how, when, and where a child will be birthed, merit reevaluation from a scriptural perspective.

Far from being a neutral area of life, the issues of labor and delivery, and the customary practices routinely followed, will either reflect the wisdom of God's created order or they will reflect a humanistic makeover of that order. Too few prospective parents have examined these issues from the Word of God and have uncritically assumed the validity of letting modern medical science practitioners make decisions for them, usually within a framework that sees childbirth as a pathology rather than a reflection of God's creative wisdom. To fully bring all areas of life and thought under the dominion of Jesus Christ, we need to recover a better-informed Biblical mindset concerning childbirth so that family prerogatives aren't surrendered to approaches that may be inconsistent with God's Word.

TRAVAIL

The Bible uses the word *travail* to describe the process of a child leaving the womb. Webster's 1828 dictionary defines this word as follows:

> *travail*, v.i. [L. trans, over, beyond, and mael, work; Eng. moil.]
> 1. To labor with pain; to toil.
> 2. To suffer the pangs of childbirth; to be in labor. (Gen. 35.)
>
> *travail*, n. Labor with pain; severe toil.
> 1. Labor in childbirth; as a severe travail; an easy travail.

In Genesis 3:16a, God promises Eve that He will "greatly multiply thy sorrow and thy conception; in sorrow thou shalt bring forth children." This is a direct response to Eve's disobedience. The Bible consistently associates pain with childbearing. In fact, the pain it-self is due to Eve's rebellion against God. It should be noted that the Scripture does not contain any directive for women to avoid this pain through the use of anesthetics.[2] These facts, while not decisive in themselves, do steer us to inquire further. First Timothy 2:14–15 reads:

> *And Adam was not deceived, but the woman being deceived was in the transgression. Notwithstanding she shall be saved in childbearing, if they continue in faith and charity and holiness with sobriety.*

One of the three most plausible interpretations of Paul's mean-ing is that these verses promise that a woman will make it through childbirth if she remains in faith, charity, holiness, and sobriety. By implication, if she embraces the calling God has given her as a wom-an, wife, and mother, she will obtain favor from the Lord. Under this interpretation, we note that Paul gave no indication that she should seek to avoid this reality of travailing, nor sedate herself during the experience. While an argument from silence has limited validity, and the interpretation is not conclusively settled, the issue surely warrants thoughtful exploration given its importance.

Eve, by her own admission (Gen. 3:13b), was deceived, specifically about the question of authority, God's authority, and invoked human wisdom in her bid to settle the question. This question of authority is a continuing factor in women's lives, and we've seen the ugly results when the state expects parents to bend to its alleged authority over education. In a like manner, women continue to bend to medical au-thorities relating to pregnancy and birth because the alternatives (like homeschooling to statist education) are routinely ridiculed. Faulty ap-peal to authority is a logical fallacy, and perhaps it's not going too far beyond the evidence to suggest that in our day women have continued to be deceived about their prerogatives concerning parenting *from the very beginning of that process*, including childbirth and the travail as-sociated with it.

---

2   It should also be noted that Proverbs 31:6–7 advises the use of an anesthetic for those in pain and dying. However, this passage is in no way connected to the process of giv-ing birth.

No Pain, No Gain?

One young mother[3] described it this way, "I think the pain is meant to remind a woman of what happens when she lives life on her own terms, and that should make her even more determined to raise that baby she has just delivered to live life on God's terms." Thus, rather than being "bad" pain, this is useful pain. Pain that will help her "count the cost" of the endeavor before her to raise her child "in the nurture and admonition of the Lord." While this is anecdotal evidence, not an explicit appeal to Scripture, it is representative of a different way of thinking about childbirth that bears further scrutiny.

Another reference to childbirth is made by Jesus in John 16:20–21:

> *Verily, verily, I say unto you, That ye shall weep and lament, but the world shall rejoice: and ye shall be sorrowful, but your sorrow shall be turned into joy.* A woman when she is in travail hath sorrow, *because her hour is come: but as soon as she is delivered of the child, she remembereth no more the anguish, for joy that a man is born into the world. [Emphasis mine.]*

Jesus, by way of analogy, is telling His disciples that their sorrow at His death will be turned to joy in His resurrection. How does He convey this? He does so by using the analogy of a woman in childbirth. This flies in the face of modern obstetrical practice that encourages pain medication to lessen the experience. Certainly we cannot imagine that Jesus was recommending that His disciples drug themselves to avoid the terrible sorrow His death would usher in for them. No, He was advocating that they parallel the normal experience of labor and resulting birth, in order to fully experience and appreciate the process by which salvation was to be ushered in for them.

---

3   Thanks to Mrs. Mike (Nicki) O'Donovan for our conversations together on this topic.

Time for a More Biblical Paradigm?

It appears that many women continue to be deceived by humanistic medical criteria in the very midst of fulfilling their respective callings to be mothers. Many mothers-to-be today buy into modern medicine's disdain for God's natural, physiological processes, and in essence agree that God's design is inherently defective. Systematic deceptions under color of medical authority include its glowing characterization of the travesty of abortion. So many women are grossly deceived when it comes to believing the lie that abortion is safe, easy, and will allow them to get on with the rest of their lives without any negative consequences. The medical profession has made a practice of telling women what they wish to hear.[4]

Assuming that most practitioners in the field of obstetrics don't harbor bad intentions toward women,[5] it remains that if their basis for pharmacological and surgical intervention is based upon humanistic principles (i.e., all pain is bad and should be reduced or avoided at all costs), women may well be deprived of the promise of their anguish being turned to joy. While it is true that the use of medications and interventions can remove a woman's memory of birth[6] or possibly reduce her pain, our Lord's comments in John 16:21 suggest that the child's arrival in the world is itself the medicine that erases the memory of the prior anguish.

While there are many voices advocating for less medical intervention and calling for natural childbirth, most are expressing their concerns on the basis of human rights abuses against women and the joy of an unmedicated birth. While there is some merit to these perspectives, they make their case on secular rather than Biblical grounds. As Christians we need to examine the "accepted" practices of natural childbirth with the purpose of attempting to develop the contours of a systematic theology as it applies to childbearing while allowing for a variety of individual applications.[7]

---

4   For personal testimonies as to the long-term effects of abortion on women, see the DVD, "Life after Abortion," http://vimeo.com/11510410

5   This is not to say that there are not legitimate circumstances where medical interventions are lifesavers for mothers and their babies.

6   See the Appendix to this book by Jo Loomis.

7   R. J. Rushdoony in his twelve Medical Reports (published in *The Roots of Reconstruction*) is a useful starting point for further examination of modern medicine by those

CONCLUSION

The so-called "experts" in the field of obstetrical practice desire that families do minimal thinking on their own and submit to the superior wisdom of modern medical science. However, as the homeschooling movement has thoroughly demonstrated, matters that are properly in the jurisdiction of families and responsibly carried out by the family bring tremendous personal and culture-changing effects.

Rushdoony points out that childbirth occurs within an ongoing context when he notes,

> It is obvious, of course, that procreation...birth, is a function of the family, and, in a healthy, biblically oriented and governed family system, this function is preceded by an important fact that conditions birth. The parents marry because there is a bond of faith and love between them, a resolution to maintain for life a covenant under God. As a result, heredity of faith and a unity in terms of it are established as a prior condition of birth, so that a child born into such a family has an inheritance which cannot be duplicated. The Biblical family cannot be rivaled by man's science or imagination as the institution for procreation and rearing of children.[8]

---

committed to the authority of Scripture.

8   R. J. Rushdoony, *Law & Liberty* (Vallecito, CA: Ross House Books), 100.

7

How Natural is Childbirth?

"Natural" childbirth came into fashion in the 1970s with the practice of husbands or other support persons being present during the labor and birth of their children while assuming the role of labor coach and companion for the birthing mother. Many heralded this as a great advance, and hospitals began to provide nicely decorated birthing rooms so that women could labor and deliver their babies in an atmosphere much closer to a bedroom than a hospital room. Previous hospital practice had involved a woman being moved to a delivery room once she had dilated fully, so this was a big change. The hope was that women would regain the capacity to deliver babies without unnecessary interventions, as they were deemed to be detrimental to both mother and baby. The idea was to let nature take its course.

One would expect that this change would have established "natural childbirth" as the norm, rather than the exception; allowing a woman to have someone of her choosing present was supposed to be a sure way to relax and comfort her. However, there has been an *increase* in the number of women requesting non-emergency medical interventions during the process of laboring, resulting in an increase in the use of electronic fetal monitoring (to note the vital signs of the baby in utero), epidurals (spinal medication used to numb the woman from the waist down), Pitocin (a synthetic form of the hormone oxytocin to speed up the first stage of labor), rupturing of membranes (in cases where the amniotic sac has not done so spontaneously), episiotomies (a surgical cut to expand the opening from which the baby passes), and cesarean sections (major surgery to deliver a baby in place of vaginal delivery).

The first issue that needs to be addressed is why these interventions are best avoided. If in the end it doesn't matter *how* a baby is born, just *that* it is born, why make this a concern at all?

Simply put, these interventions have consequences for the long-term relationship between mother and child. Because today there is an unrealistic expectation on the part of parents and medical personnel as to how long labor should take, especially a first labor, the many "helps" that are available from the hospital "pain reduction" menu often are the very factors that lead to eventual C-sections.

Michel Odent, a French obstetrician, gets to the heart of the matter when he says,

> Oxytocin is the hormone of love, and to give birth without releasing this complex cocktail of love chemicals disturbs the first contact between the mother and the baby. The hormone is produced during sex and breastfeeding, as well as birth, but in the moments after birth, a woman's oxytocin level is the highest it will ever be in her life, and this peak is vital. It is this hormone flood that enables a woman to fall in love with her newborn and forget the pain of birth.

What we can say for sure is that when a woman gives birth with a pre-labour Caesarean section she does not release this flow of love hormones, so she is a different woman than if she had given birth naturally and the first contact between mother and baby is different.[1]

As it turned out, the push for natural childbirth didn't materialize into a significant change. The woman still was placed in a bed on her back with feet in stirrups, a very unnatural position for giving birth. That in itself intensifies the pain and lengthens the labor. Given these "accepted practices," over time women resorted to the pain meds that were readily offered as the only way to endure.

Add to that the artificial time schedule assigned to "normal" labor that made it so birth had to occur at the convenience of the hospital

---

1   Quoted in Emily Cook, "Women who have Caesarean's less likely to bond,'" Mail Online, July 13, 2006, http://www.dailymail.co.uk/health/article-395218/Women-Caesareans-likely-bond.html#ixzz1Oi15Fyh6. Dr. Odent was speaking at a conference sponsored by an educational charity promoting a holistic approach to pregnancy, birth, and babyhood.

staff, who would have a tendency to rush things along if a shift change were approaching, or to accommodate a doctor's schedule, or should there be a need for the hospital bed.

So, what happened to the *natural* part of childbirth? What does the term even mean?

NATURAL CHILDBIRTH

Obstetrician Grantly Dick-Read is credited with coining the term "natural childbirth," which he used in his books *Natural Childbirth* (1933) and *Childbirth Without Fear* (1944). His philosophy centers on the idea that women are innately able to give birth to children, without external intervention. He took a stand against the pathological model modern medicine had adopted, and he feared practitioners were rapidly forgetting what a *normal* birth even looked like.

> One of the most important factors in the production of complicated labour and therefore of maternal and infantile morbidity, is the inability of obstetricians and midwives to stand by and allow the natural and uninterrupted course of labour. It may be an excess of zeal, or anxiety born of ignorance, but it is an unquestionable fact that interference is still one of the greatest dangers with which both mother and child have to contend.[2]

Dick-Read was addressing what Dr. Jo Loomis (see Appendix) categorized as the shift that occurred in the practice of childbearing in the West in the early part of the twentieth century. The routine practice of homebirth attended by a midwife had given way to obstetricians (surgeons) and nurses overseeing the birthing process in hospital settings.

Had adopting the hospital model caused women to lose their innate instincts of how to give birth? Had the shift in thinking pro-

---

2   Peter Dunn, "Perinatal Lessons from the Past," Archives of Disease in Childhood 1994; 71: F145-F146, accessed via http://www.ncbi.nlm.nih.gov/pmc/articles/PMC1061103/pdf/ archdischfn00037-0073.pdf.

duced a generation of women who wanted "natural childbirth" but found it difficult to proceed because their own perspective (as well as the hospital's perspective) of "natural childbirth" lacked a full understanding of the process? Was it inevitable that the trend toward natural childbirth would give way to the practice of unnecessary medical interventions?

Dick-Read sized up the situation back in the '30s and '40s:

> Woman … is adapted primarily for the perfection of womanhood which is, according to the law of Nature, reproduction. All that is most beautiful in her life is associated with the emotions leading up to this ultimate function. But unfortunately in the final perfection of these joys a large majority remember only the pain and anguish and even terror that they were called upon to endure at the birth of their first child. That is indeed a paradox. For generations, childbirth has been accepted as a dangerous and painful experience.[3]

He noted that medicine had placed too much focus in the direction of pharmaceutical relief, and not enough emphasis on adequately preparing women for the birthing process.

> Obstetric teaching has made great advances in the use of drugs, analgesics and anaesthetics, but little has been done to investigate the problem of pain from the point of view of its preclusion … Anything that disturbs the confidence and peacefulness of the mother disrupts the neuromuscular harmony of her labour … In childbirth, fear and the anticipation of pain give rise to natural protective tensions in the body.
>
> Unfortunately, the natural muscular tension produced by fear also influences the muscles that close the womb and thus delay the progress of the labour and create pain … The safest and most effective way to minimise the discomforts of childbirth is to enable a woman, by preparation for, and understanding attention at labour to have her baby

---

3   Dunn, "Perinatal Lessons."

naturally...Education and antenatal instruction are important factors in the relief of pain in childbirth.[4]

A SYSTEMATIC THEOLOGY OF CHILDBIRTH

In Chapter 6, I explore what the Bible has to say about labor, pointing out that the travail of childbirth is an important component for women becoming committed to the task of motherhood. Jesus's analogy to His apostles concerning their future sadness at His death being turned to joy at His resurrection drew comparisons to the process of labor and delivery, with the apparent implication that this travail was not something to be avoided (John 16:21) but rather one that would actually result in an exuberant outcome.[5]

Dick-Read made the observation based on his experience:

> It is my custom to lift up the crying child even before the cord is cut so that the mother may see ... the reality of her dreams ... the first to grasp the small fingers and touch gingerly the soft skin of the infant's cheek ... Its first cry remains an indelible memory on the mind of a mother ... No mother and no child should be denied that great mystical association ... it lays a foundation of unity of both body and spirit upon which the whole edifice of mother love stands. Many times I have called attention to the wonderful picture of pure ecstasy that we see at a natural birth ... Is it just an accident that the brilliant sunlight of motherhood breaks through and dispels for all time the clouds of her labour? No change in human emotions is more dramatic ... Such an aura of beauty has filled the whole atmosphere of the room and such superhuman loveliness has swept over the features of the girl whose baby is crying in her hands ... I have experienced a sense of happiness

---

4   Ibid.
5   This is in no way to posit that childbirth must be excruciatingly painful in order for it to be handled in a scriptural fashion, given the limited weight we can attach to any arguments drawn from an analogy.

myself much more akin to reverence and awe than to the simple satisfaction of just another natural birth.[6]

On its face, then, John 16:21 seems quite compatible with this firsthand observation by an experienced practitioner. In that light, it would seem to follow that to achieve the God-intended bond between mother and child, the first prerequisite to a "good labor" is for the mother to be spiritually prepared and bolstered for what lies ahead.

There are numerous Bible passages that speak to the reality that bringing a child into the world is not without intense emotion and physical discomfort (Rev. 12:2; Isa. 13:8, 21:3, 37:3). Given the concomitant realities—intense physical, often painful, exertion followed by equally intense emotional exuberance—women are well advised to look to additional passages of Scripture that, while not expressly written to a woman in labor, have a fitting general application to her estate as she moves through the normal stages of labor that culminate in the delivery of her child.

> *Come to Me, all you who labor and are heavy laden, and I will give you rest. Take My yoke upon you, and learn from Me, for I am gentle and lowly in heart, and you will find rest for your souls. For My yoke is easy and My burden is light.* (Matt. 11:28–30 NKJV)
>
> *Yea, though I walk through the valley of the shadow of death, I will fear no evil; for You are with me; Your rod and Your staff, they comfort me* (Ps. 23:4 NKJV)
>
> *Cast your burden on the LORD, and He shall sustain you; He shall never permit the righteous to be moved.* (Ps. 55:22 NKJV)

As with every area of life and thought, approaching childbirth with the most Biblical mindset we can muster will surely maximize the blessings God intends for His people.

---

6   Dunn, "Perinatal Lessons."

The Husband's Dilemma

Dick-Read, in positing a better way to approach the process of child-bearing and birth, noted,

> I never left any woman alone during labour, a prey to the destructive forces of uncontrolled imagination. If I could not be there myself from the start, I made sure that some-one was with her—her husband, mother, or sister, to whom I had already given a little instruction on what to expect.[7]

So, the resurgence of natural childbirth practices proved correct in attempting to create a safe, secure environment for the birthing woman, but some unexpected results came about with the introduction of the husband into the process.

Partly due to the breakdown of the trustee family, many couples in the '70s and '80s were living within the atomistic framework of family life. Women who wanted their mothers or other mother-like figures present were few and far between, and the hospital nurse, often a new acquaintance, was the major support a woman received. That left the husband to fulfill a role that over the centuries usually fell to doulas and midwives, women with the position and experience to bolster a woman through successful labor and delivery. Most men would readily admit that they are at a deficit when it comes to achieving an authentic understanding of all the changes that begin for a woman at the outset of pregnancy all the way to delivery. The calm that is needed is one that is not a natural response to seeing the woman they love in such apparent pain.

Michel Odent, an obstetrician with thousands of births to his credit, points out that the last thing a woman in labor needs is adrenaline—her own or that of her support person. Adrenaline is a combatant to oxytocin, the hormone that is at play to encourage contractions and bring about a narcotic type relief between them. According to Odent, often the husband, inadvertently, produces such an adrenaline response that he lengthens her labor considerably.

Peter Dunn, in his paper for the National Institutes of Health, summarizes Dick-Read's observations after Dick-Read had spent a

---

7   Ibid.

considerable amount of time traveling throughout Africa in 1948. Through his travels, he discovered that childbirth was not a forgotten skill among the women he encountered.

> [Dick-Read] found that well over 90 per cent of women in the tribes he visited had normal, natural births and needed no more convalescence than a few hours' rest. He noted how they automatically adopted an upright position which made passage through the birth canal both safer and easier for the child. He observed that in most tribes the mother was well instructed in the course of labour by old women in whom she had complete confidence and that she was never left alone when in labour. It was particularly interesting to him to see at first hand the profound respect that every tribe had for the afterbirth and the manner of its delivery. Again, any interference with the work of nature was banned. A child was never separated from the placenta until that structure had been delivered. Only then might the cord be cut and the offspring delivered into its mother's embrace.[8]

The Ultimate Athletic Event

Consider the woman who is pregnant with her first child. It is an understatement to say everything is new for her. Contrast her with a woman who is pregnant for a second or third time. This woman's body has already undergone delivery; she has a greater sense of the marathon before her, and has previously experienced the joy of holding, nursing, and loving the child she labored over.

Since every woman's birthing experience will be unique to her, physical, mental, and spiritual preparation is of vital importance, especially if she has to combat the images she's seen in film and television depictions of screaming, out-of-control women.[9]

---

8   Dunn, "Perinatal Lessons."

9   A recent Lifetime Channel series called "One Born Every Minute" gave such a lopsided view of labor, to the point that in their opening trailer, woman after woman

Having a mentor, an experienced doula, or midwife helping her maneuver her way through this strenuous, athletic process enables her to remain focused on the task at hand, not getting too far ahead of herself and taking each contraction as it comes, without a predetermined agenda for how long her labor should take.

Dick-Read, in the preface to the fourth edition (1959) of *Childbirth Without Fear*, speaks to the importance of approaching the birth of a baby with reverence and respect.

> [C]hildbirth is fundamentally a spiritual as well as physical achievement and throughout this book it must be read and understood that the birth of a child is the ultimate perfection of human love. In the Christian ethic we teach that God is love in which the blessing of sexual necessity and pleasure is but an essential part. Obstetrics must be approached as a science demanding the most profound respect. It must maintain the poise and dignity of those whose estimate of values finds a place for all types and variations of women. It demands cheerfulness without frivolity and sacrifice without reward, for of itself no guerdon could be greater than the gratitude of those whom we are privileged to serve.
>
> I am persuaded from long years of experience amongst women of many nationalities that good midwifery is essential for the true happiness of motherhood—that good midwifery is the birth of a baby in a manner nearest to the natural law and design—and good midwifery, next to wise and healthy pregnancy, sets the pattern of the newborn infant and its relationship to its mother.
>
> For this sequence a sound and stable philosophy is a basic necessity. Materialism and atheism are not included in the make-up of motherhood. Neither can a robot lead a blind man across the road.[10]

---

is shown screaming and groaning. Repeatedly, nurses offered epidurals the way waitresses offer water to restaurant customers. It was expected that women would want and need one.

10 Grantly Dick-Read, *Childbirth Without Fear*, Appendix: Preface to the Fourth Edition (1959), 568-577.

Conclusion

Michel Odent, a strong proponent of gentle birth, points out the irony that if non-emergency medical interventions were to stop altogether, many women and children today would be put at risk—not because C-sections and other standard medical practices are good for mother or baby in the long term, but rather because women have lost their innate capacity to travail through the normal birthing process and need to learn how to regain that skill.[11]

Why have Western women seemingly lost the ability to proceed through labor and delivery without medical interventions when women from less medically advanced cultures seem to glide through the process? Could it be that with the humanistic thrust that has dominated the West, with science determining there is no longer any need for God and His Word, that women have become convinced that their bodies are incapable of doing precisely that task God has designed them to do? From a Biblical point of view, childbirth cannot as a rule be seen as a pathology that demands massive intervention, but rather as a God-ordained process through which the command to be fruitful and multiply is to be fulfilled.

When people put their trust in materialistic philosophies in opposition to the triune God and fail to acknowledge the supremacy of Scripture over every activity and segment of life, the results are sure to be detrimental. R. J. Rushdoony hits the nail on the head when he notes,

> The growth of non-Christian materialism had led to false and rather mechanical views of medicine. If our car needs oil or gas, we add these things to the car; if we need a new fuel pump, we replace the old one. In like manner, some people expect cure-all dosages and changes and are resentful when the doctor cannot work miracles. Their ex-

---

11 "Michel Odent – on gentle birth [parts 1-3]," YouTube videos, from an interview by OWL productions, uploaded by elmerpostleowl, November 3, 2007, http://www.youtube.com/watch?v=zBjZ5rMoHkU, http://www.youtube.com/watch?v=8x8ip4VVGAI, http://www.youtube.com/watch?v=EXf1pcfKS10.

pectation, however mechanical, is still religious, but it is in essence paganism, not Biblical faith.

This, of course, is the heart of the matter. There must be a return to a Biblical view of medicine as a calling, and as a priestly-pastoral calling, but there must also be a return to Christian faith on the part of the people, or false and unreasonable demands will be made of medicine.[12]

12   R. J. Rushdoony, "Chalcedon Medical Report No. 1: The Medical Profession as a Priestly Calling," *Roots of Reconstruction* (Vallecito, CA: Ross House Books, 1991), 459-460.

8

Minimizing the Work of the Spirit

*M*any feel that young children cannot handle difficult Biblical doctrines like the doctrines of hell, eternal damnation, predestination, and election. They choose to emphasize the "more pleasant" elements of the faith, such as storing up treasures in heaven, ministering angels, and letting one's light shine. They do not want to present a "negative" view of God because they are afraid that would discourage children from choosing to follow Jesus.

However, when children do not learn early that they possess an inherited trait that puts them at enmity with God, they blissfully "float" through childhood without being aware of the spiritual dangers they face. For Christ's work to have cogent meaning for them, it is imperative that they learn in their tenderhearted years what a tremendous price was paid by Jesus for sin and that apart from Him they have no hope of rescue. Our Savior had so much confidence that children were able to receive His teachings that He presented children as examples that adults should follow as they entered the Kingdom (Mark 10:15).

The shielding of children from these strong, sobering doctrines and the reluctance of adults in children's lives to "tell it like it is" points to a greater problem, namely a serious minimizing of the power and influence of the Holy Spirit in the lives of believers. Because twenty-first-century Christendom is replete with antinomianism, easy-believism, and syncretism, many Christian parents don't expect to see the transformation of the Holy Spirit in the lives of their children. Could it be that they don't expect to see it in the lives of adults either?

THE ROOT CAUSE

Biblical doctrines of sin and grace have been so polluted and dumbed-down that they do not come close to Biblical doctrines. As Rushdoony points out in his *Systematic Theology*,

> How we view sin's effect upon us will also mark or color our view of the effects of grace and the Holy Spirit. If sin acts on the borders or peripheries of our lives, then too so will grace and the Holy Spirit. All the while, our hearts are then reserved to ourselves.[1]

If the Spirit has come, there is life, and if there is no life, it is evidence that the Spirit has not come. There is no such thing as partial regeneration. A person *is* or *is not* born again. I believe that much of the confusion regarding this topic comes from a misinterpretation of Jesus' words "you must be born again" (John 3:7).

How one understands the usage of "must" is crucial. Does "must" mean "should," the way we say, "You must obey the speed limit"? Or does "must" mean "an essential requisite," the way we say, "Your heart must be beating for you to be alive"? If we understand "must" to be "should," we place the emphasis in salvation on man's work and initiation, rather than on God's work and initiation. When Jesus told Nicodemus that he must be born again, He was not prompting or prodding Nicodemus to do anything. Jesus was not attempting to *move* Nicodemus into action; He was establishing the Spirit's prerogative in giving new life to those He chooses.

When we explain the regenerating work of the Holy Spirit (to our children or others), it is important that we not diminish or play down the totality of the resultant transformation. Rushdoony's explanation brings this to light:

> Salvation is total: we are transferred from death to life, from sin to righteousness, by the justification of God through Jesus Christ. Christ our sacrifice takes upon Himself our death penalty, and God declares that our sins are

---

1   R. J. Rushdoony, *Systematic Theology, Vol. 1* (Vallecito, CA: Ross House Books, 1994), 304.

remitted, and our legal standing before Him is as righteous men. We are saved. This does not mean our problems are over. A man snatched from a burning house and certain death has only his life; all else is gone. He must now work to establish the capital or substance of his saved life. So too the redeemed man must now put on holiness, work in obedience to God's word, to grow in terms of the new life which is his and become a rich man in grace, faith, and obedience to his Savior.[2]

A redeemed person is a *changed* individual. This fact should not be minimized. The change is not manifested in one's *profession* of faith, but in one's *evidence* of faith. When Jesus said that we will know our brothers and sisters in the faith by their fruit (Matt. 7:16), He was not being esoteric. He meant that we would know them by how they kept His law as manifested by the fruit of the Spirit—love, joy, peace, long-suffering, gentleness, goodness, faith, meekness, and temperance. These attributes are not pietistic pretentions, but rather a full-blown commitment to every word that proceeds out of the mouth of God. Good fruit is produced by keeping the law of God; antinomianism (lawlessness) is the evidence of bad fruit. As Rushdoony points out,

> [T]he summons to manifest the fruits of the Spirit is not a call to a vague and antinomian spirituality, nor to mysticism, but a summing up of the whole of God's requirements of us in His law-word. The Spirit nowhere renounces His word.[3]

By Way of Illustration

Years ago, I met Michael, an eight-year-old boy who was at Stanford Children's Hospital receiving chemotherapy treatments for non-Hodgkin's lymphoma. His situation was compounded by the fact that he had received a heart transplant seven years earlier. By the time I

---

2   Ibid., 507
3   Ibid., 371.

met him, because of chemo, he was bald, with no eyebrows or eye-lashes, and donned a mask anytime he was out in public. Michael took up to sixty meds a day to balance the competing issues of poten-tial rejection of his donated heart while doctors attempted to build up his immune system to battle the cancer. Sometimes he had some ex-treme reactions to his difficult circumstances, compounded by drug interactions, such as chasing his mother with a knife or ramming his foot into the glove compartment of the car and smashing it. Because of his delicate medical situation, normal forms of discipline were not at his parents' disposal.

I had a heart-to-heart talk with Michael. I asked if he spent any time praying that God would heal him. He was surprised at my ques-tion; he thought it evident that he wanted to be cured. I pointed out from Scripture that he was foolish to ask God for healing at the same time he was actively violating God's commandments. I read from Exodus, "Honor your father and your mother, that your days may be long upon the land which the LORD your God is giving you" (Ex. 20:12 NKJV). I told him that God considered the prayers of the disobedient an abomination (Prov. 15:8). Michael's eyes grew wide. He acknowl-edged his lack of self-control and sin of throwing temper tantrums when he did not get his way. I could see he was convicted of his sin. He got the message that he was demonstrating bad fruit. We did not discuss whether he was a Christian or not; the question I asked was, "Are you acting in accordance with your profession of faith?"

Many would question my approach of speaking to a sick child about God's condemnation. However, not only did Michael receive the correction well, he became a vocal ambassador for Jesus Christ whenever he had a hospital stay, a doctor visit, or when he was about to be put under anesthesia. Michael gained a reputation for interact-ing and consoling other patients in the hospital, and when he died eight years later, hundreds of people attended the memorial service of this young saint. Michael received the Kingdom just as Jesus said he could, and the working of the Holy Spirit in his life was unmistakable.

We should not demand verbal proofs of our children's commitment to the Lord. We need to teach them the fundamentals of the faith and communicate that their words and actions will reveal their heart's condition. When dealing with defiance and rebellion in children, it is not only important to correct the bad behavior, but we must use the incident as an opportunity to instruct how the breach was a violation of the law of God. I realize that, for some families, entire days might be spent in this correction mode, but done consistently, the training of the child will "kick in," and the infractions will diminish. By teaching the law of God and grounding the children in its application, parents are raising them up in the way they should go (Prov. 22:6). This constant tutoring to Christ is one of the main functions of the law (Gal. 3:24).

THE LAW AND THE SPIRIT

In today's world, it is unfashionable to question someone's faith based on his works, yet the Scripture tells us that faith without works is dead (James 2:20). In addition, the charge of legalism is often levied against those who assert that God's law-word is binding on all men at all times.

> St. Paul is emphatically making clear the connection between the Holy Spirit, the law of God, and the spiritual man. Thus, where the Holy Spirit is at work, the law of God is the delight of the spiritual man, and, where men resist or despise the Spirit, they resist and despise the law given by that Spirit.[4]

Our world is full of people who have never been taught Biblical faith and who have been offered an outwardly appealing counterfeit. We must be sure that we do not cheapen the meaning of grace by coaxing or cajoling people to "accept" something they have no power or ability to conjure up on their own. Rather, our task is to present truth unequivocally and help our listeners understand that although all men are born under condemnation, responding to the message of the gospel is proof of the call of the Holy Spirit.[5]

---

4   Ibid., 359.
5   This is the balance that affirms the prerogative of God in election and at the same time does not diminish the culpability of men in their rebellion.

Too often, we pass over the powerful words of Scripture and mini-mize their meanings. Second Corinthians 5:17 makes a bold state-ment,

> *Therefore if any man be in Christ, he is a new creature: old*
> *things are passed away; behold, all things are become new.*

The tenderhearted child is not only ready to receive the Word, but has a receptivity that should not be bypassed. As parents teach their children about the miracle of being born again, children will develop a longing and desire to have what their parents have described. Of course, if these truths are not presented with conviction, children may consider these truths to be merely fairy tales. Consider the ex-pectation of hearing the promise of Acts 1:8,

> *But you shall receive power when the Holy Spirit has come*
> *upon you; and you shall be my witnesses in Jerusalem, and*
> *in all Judea and Samaria, and to the end of the earth.* (NKJV)

That power is the power to put on the full armor of God, the power to stand against the wiles of the devil, the power to recognize that when temptations abound, God promises a way out (1 Cor. 10:13). This is the good news of the gospel.

However, the good news does not stop there. We need to embrace our identity as *more than conquerors* (Rom. 8:37), and we should ex-pect to witness the life-changing effects of salvation. Counterfeit por-trayals of conversion (faith and repentance) only serve to slander the Holy Spirit. We then somehow have to reconcile lawless behavior as being consistent with the indwelling of the Third Person of the Trin-ity. Once this compromise is made in our thinking, believers begin to expect less, and our resultant Kingdom work is crippled.

Don't Settle for Less

Too much emphasis is placed on our experience or human perspective when it comes to our conversion, and we regularly see manifestations of this sorry substitute. Spending inordinate amounts of time rehearsing the circumstances of one's conversion or life prior to faith is very much majoring on the minors.

> A man may or may not know the day of his conversion; he cannot know when God regenerated him; but he cannot escape knowing that he is regenerated and converted. It is the same as knowing that we are alive, only now alive in Christ.[6]

As believers grow in grace (sanctification), their nature is renewed and remade after the image of God. This is a process but not a hidden one. Where holiness—the process of being sanctified—develops, there also develops a desire to be led by God's Spirit *according* to His Word. Believers are no longer generating sin at their core,[7] but are moving in holiness (obedience of faith to the law). Children need to understand that the mark of their allegiance is not only in what they do not do, but also in what they deliberately do.

As converts embrace and exude the righteousness (justice) of God throughout every facet of their being, startling changes take place in their lives and in their efforts. They possess the *power* of the Holy Spirit within them, no small matter. The miracle of the Third Person of the Trinity making His abode within His people should not be reduced to pietistic and charismatic manifestations. So much of the meaning of Pentecost and our own baptism of the Holy Spirit is lost when we fail to grasp the fuller implications. Rushdoony explains,

> Pentecost was thus a coronation, not of believers collectively as a church, but as individuals who are members of Christ. We are told of the glory, "and it sat upon each of them." In the world of Christ's day, where the meaning of the royal flame was well known, the meaning of Pentecost was clear: the glory of God was given, not to the kings

---

6 Rushdoony, 534.

7 The unbeliever is guilty of *anomia*, a dedicated rebellion against God's law. The believer, while not fully sanctified this side of heaven, still sins (*hamartia*), but his sin is more indicative of missing the mark rather than aiming to miss.

and emperors of the world, but to covenant man, redeemed man.[8]

The meaning thus of the flames of Pentecost is that we put on Jesus Christ as our glorification. The emphasis is not on our experience, but on our relationship and obedience to Jesus Christ, God's manifest glory.[9]

This is the substance of our faith, that we abide in Christ and He abides in us. We are His friends if we do whatsoever He commands us, and we bear His glory when we keep His commandments or law.[10] In this way, we manifest our positional standing according to our royal lineage. This is not too difficult for children who have been taught the implications of faith in Christ. But because we expect so much less, we are not concerned when we see little fruit.

As we appreciate the glorious benefits we have been given, we need to avoid viewing salvation from a man-centered perspective. Rather, we are to see it in terms of God's purpose for the establishment and furtherance of His Kingdom. We are released from our slavery to sin and death and empowered for service to the Lord.[11] Much more than dwelling on our inner feelings, repeatedly rehearsing our life circumstances prior to conversion, or dwelling on and cataloguing the blessings we have received, our salvation calls us to service. The Gospel account of Jesus' words to Peter, as recounted in John 21:15–17, shows that Christ was more concerned with His call on Peter's life than discussing the inner feelings and regrets of Peter's denial.

An emotional confession, and comforting words from Christ, would have left Peter and all the betraying band of apostles feeling better. Our Lord prevented this. He gave them a task, because the redeemed and forgiven people of God are not called to concentrate on their feelings and conditions but to serve the Lord with gladness. Peter's calling was the mark of grace and forgiveness. The forgiven do not dwell on the past, nor on their sins: Christ has dealt

---

8   Rushdoony, 552.
9   Ibid., 555.
10 Ibid.
11 Ibid., 561.

with their sins, and they stand forgiven and redeemed. Their sins are the dead past, but their calling is the present and future.[12]

Expecting the Holy Spirit to empower us as we live according to God's Word is the prerequisite for unabashed dominion and Kingdom work. Jesus told us that Spirit-driven faith would allow us to move mountains. God knows that there are some big ones to move in our day! How our children transform the culture we leave them will be determined by their dominion-oriented response to the Holy Spirit. We need not hold back; they can handle it!

---

12   Ibid.

9

Eternity in their Hearts

One of the many evil byproducts of the Prussian system of education that has been embraced by our public schools is a system of grades.[1] This artificial designation takes children from the family, groups all children of a certain age into one class and teaches them from a stagnant curriculum, designed by experts for that age group, not taking into consideration the personal development or skills of the individual child.[2]

Because this system has been a part of America's educational system for so long, parents often ignore their own observations and gut instincts regarding their child and accept all sorts of diagnoses presented by the public school experts who say the child is a slow learner, has ADD or ADHD, or is dyslexic, and so on. The diagnosing of these children is based on a godless system of psychology that sees the child not as an image-bearer of God but as an animal that can be trained and manipulated. This philosophy retards the child from developing into all that he can be under godly nurture. Many children have suffered much harm as a result of being so labeled by public school authorities.

In accepting these labels, parents defer to the realm of psychology in place of Biblical Christianity, because a Biblical psychology is not taught in public schools or from our pulpits.

---

1   The Prussian system of education was a godless system that trained children to become beneficial servants of the state instead of nurturing their God-given talents for His service.

2   Homeschooling has debunked this contrivance inasmuch as it allows a child to learn at his own pace and examines understanding as a prerequisite to "moving on" with his studies, rather than cheapen learning with the concept of merely "passing."

Rushdoony notes,

> Humanistic psychology gives us a doctrine of man radi-
> cally at odds with Scripture. It has become routine for cler-
> gymen to look to humanistic psychologies for guidance in
> pastoral counseling, and books applying such psychologies
> to pastoral problems have a ready market and widespread
> influence. The result has been the steady infiltration of
> humanism into Christian circles and the steady erosion of
> the Biblical doctrines of man and salvation.[3]

Psychology is properly categorized as a branch of theology. It concerns itself with man's nature and inner life, the realm of the soul
or the mind.[4] The doctrine of man as laid out in Scripture begins
and ends with man as a creature. Sin is what polluted God's creation
and only God's remedy (salvation through Jesus Christ) repairs the
breach. To leave children in the hands of humanistic psychology and
its practitioners in public schools and elsewhere results in a warped
view of children and numerous ungodly ways to relate to them.

Rushdoony makes it clear,

> Man was created a mature being, not a child. This is a
> fact of central importance. We cannot make child psychol-
> ogy basic to an understanding of man …
>
> If man in his origin is a product of a long evolutionary
> past, man is then best understood in terms of the animal,
> the savage, and the child. However, since man was in his
> origin a mature creation, his psychology is best understood
> in terms of that fact. Man's sins and shortcomings rep-
> resent not a lingering primitivism or a reversion to child-
> hood, but rather a deliberate revolt against maturity and
> the requirements of maturity. By ascribing to man, as hu-
> manistic psychologies do, a basic substratum of primitiv-
> ism and racial childishness, this *revolt against maturity* is

---

3   R. J. Rushdoony, *Revolt Against Maturity* (Vallecito, CA: Ross House Books, 1987), 5.
4   Ibid., 1.

given an ideological justification; the studied and maturely developed immaturity of man is encouraged and justified.[5]

Biblical nurturing is based on the development of the child, recognizing what he is capable of at each stage of development, and customizing training based on the individual. This nurturing must be grounded in the reality that,

> The child is not only a person but a concept; in that each culture has its own particular idea and expectation of a child … The child is born into a culture and is loved and honored as it meets the expectations of that culture.[6]

Christians need to adopt expectations for their children based on Scriptural principles. What follows is intended to encourage parents to think outside the pagan, psychological and educational box.

STAGES OF CHILDHOOD

Newborns

The Biblical view of children is that they are a blessing from the Lord (Psalm 127). That doesn't mean they are sinless. A proper understanding of the Fall and the need for atonement must be among the first lessons parents impart to their infant children. How parents deal with a newborn should reflect that, however innocent the child may appear, sin is part of the equation. Everything the parent (or caregivers, be they grandparents or siblings) does for the child must be in this context. Does that mean a crying baby is manifesting deliberate wickedness? Certainly not. But the child is demonstrating a self-centeredness that includes the attitude, "I don't like what is going on and I want what I want when I want it!"

---

5   Ibid., 6.
6   R. J. Rushdoony, *Intellectual Schizophrenia* (Vallecito, CA: Ross House Books, [1961] 2002), 73.

Rushdoony notes that since man was created in the image of God, man must live by revelation. He states, "Every fiber of his being must respond to God's law for its health."[7] Thus, from the outset, a mother must instill in her child the reality of God's law-word, purposefully framing all her interactions with her infant accordingly. Feedings, diaper changes, and naptimes should be opportunities to speak to her baby the truths of Scripture, knowing that although the child may not comprehend all the words, he will respond to the emotional context in which they are spoken. What a blessing to be able to say there was never a time in his life where the Word of God was absent!

Babies

There is a point when a child goes from being a "new" baby to just being a baby. It is at this stage where there is some recognition by the child that there are boundaries. It's easy to tell when this occurs because there is a more urgent necessity to communicate the concept of *No!* in order to keep the child safe. However, the use of the word *No* should always have included with it an explanation. The parental retort, "Because I told you so" is not Biblical. If the parent's authority doesn't come from God, the parent does not have legitimate authority.[8] If interactions with the child are grounded in Scripture, then there will be no need for this refrain, because the child will be aware that the parents' requirements are in terms of God's Word.

For example: "Stop crying," is better expressed, "Crying will not bring your food any sooner. You must learn to be patient. The Bible states ..." If the mother is faithful to teach this during the many opportunities to deal with a sobbing baby, the child will learn that he does not set the agenda for the household. Care should be taken to treat tantrums and outbursts as futile efforts on the part of the child to gain control. Again, although the child may not understand the full meaning of the words spoken, when communicated properly the intent will be understood.

---

7   R. J. Rushdoony, *Revolt Against Maturity* (Vallecito, CA: Ross House Books, 1987), 9.
8   See Chapter 5, "The Expectation of Children.".

Young Children

When children leave the baby stage they become aware of their new abilities, and thus test boundaries. Mobility and language propel the child into entirely new arenas of life. It is at this point that the mother's work escalates and she earns her stripes. Catechism memorization (teaching the doctrines of the faith) is a fundamental step in stewarding a child's life. Parents need to establish the foundation upon which their household runs (Josh. 24:15), and regularly evaluate their family policies and practices to ensure that they haven't strayed off the "straight and narrow path." By establishing the foundation for obedience, transgressions can be dealt with in terms of repentance and forgiveness.

Older Children

Responsibility is the key ingredient in determining when your children fit into the category of "older children." Rather than rely on the artificial method of *grades* or even age, the criteria should include how well your son or daughter responds to instruction and family guidelines within the context of God's law-word. This may be different with every child in the family. If the earlier paths have been properly travelled, the family gains a tremendous asset as these members move beyond being total dependents to active participants in the life of the family.[9]

MOTIVATION

In each of these stages of growth, motivation plays an essential part. Tied into the concept of motivation is that of incentivizing behavior.

---

9   Some decry the practice of older brothers and sisters taking on significant responsibilities with their younger siblings in the areas of care and schooling. This is a direct result of failing to view the family as God's primary institution. What is so sad when it comes to Christian families making use of public schools to educate their children is that children become conditioned to believe that school teachers and classmates/peers are their best allies and where their responsibilities lie.

Just as most adults don't pursue certain activities without a reason or compensation (*most wouldn't show up for a job if a paycheck was not part of the deal*), children need to be dealt with in terms of payment or reward. I am not talking about bribery. I'm referring to the intrinsic need to be working toward a goal with purpose. By failing to establish this, children can easily become bored, time wasters, or mischievous. Even Jesus promised rewards in heaven (Matt. 6:20) as an incentive for faithfulness.

Some children seemingly start off in life with a strong desire to please and this makes it much easier to spend time with them. However, if pleasing others becomes paramount rather than obedience to God's Word, then it is likely that the child will learn how to adapt to anyone in authority and become pragmatic in his actions and decisions. Instilling in children a desire to "fear God and keep His commandments" will also unearth those particular gifts and abilities that God has placed in each individual child. When these surface, proper incentive and motivation become much easier to practice.

That said, not all children approach life this way and parents must continue to inculcate in their more *difficult* children a sense of duty and responsibility that trumps their particular desires or whims. The message is the same, regardless of the temperament of the child, but requires a bit more consistency with those who seem to fight at every turn.

It might be helpful at this point to illustrate the concept of providing an incentive or motivation in some of the more mundane aspects of family life.

SHOE-TYING

Each of my children struggled with this maneuver. By knowing them as individuals, I was able to appeal to "what made them tick" in order to help them succeed. With my son, who refused to take responsibility for a task he was quite capable of completing, it took an ultimatum on a Friday afternoon. I informed him that he was going to miss participating in the Saturday soccer game if he was unable to tie his own cleats. Rather than fight with him, I told him that we would find other things to do with our Saturday morning—maybe even sleep in. Now, he needed my help, and rather than being resistive, he was motivated to receive instruction. I didn't make a threat; I promised him a consequence. In this way I was treating him as God treats His children: blessings for obedience and penalties for disobedience.

In my youngest daughter's case, her inability to perform this task had more to do with her tendency to act as though she understood the instructions of her father, when she really was quite lost. Because her dad didn't understand this character flaw in his daughter, he would become frustrated and assume she was being deliberately disobedient. He would get angry and she would cry. It was a vicious circle. I was able to mediate the situation finally by promising her that by that day's end, she *would* know how to tie her shoes. She remembers the episode vividly: I broke the process down into simple steps, encouraging her as she repeated each one over and over. By the time we were nearing the end, she'd say, "I can do it all now." I would tell her not to jump ahead and keep doing the earlier steps. By the time her dad came home, she met him at the door with a big smile and said, "Watch this!" I was just imitating our God who teaches us line upon line, precept upon precept.

A Sick Child

Parents often dread the scenario of dealing with a sick child. Pushing liquids gets to be a chore and a source of confrontation at a time when neither mom nor child needs a fight. Instead of fighting and threatening punishment, I endeavored to get my children to enjoy the process. So, depending on the child, I would take a ball point pen and draw a bunny or a cat or a puppy on their tummies. I would tell them that the bunny was thirsty and it was time to give it a drink. If they hesitated, I would make a whimpering sound and let them know that he was crying. They would take a sip from the straw and sometimes I would catch them taking an extra sip *just to be nice!*

I would do the same thing with the wearing of seatbelts in the car. Rather than make it a police action, we would have seatbelt races. Each child wanted to be declared the winner, and I would often "lose." The result was that I was able to get cooperation rather than a fight by orchestrating what would bring about the result I wanted.

FINDING ONE'S CALLING

I used to tell my children that they didn't have to search too hard for what God was calling them to do. As young ones in a family, they arrived with the duty to be a son or a daughter, a sister or a brother. As they matured, the role of student was added to the "job description." As they learned and experienced many facets of growth (academics, music, arts, athletics, and service) certain assessments were made by them of things they enjoyed and wanted to pursue. From a parental viewpoint, I found it important to show them *how* to hear God's specific call, rather than rely on me to announce it. I used to say, "God won't leave a message for you on my answering machine."

It is here when the paradigm of grade levels and judgments based on age can be detrimental. If we approach all four-year-olds the same way, determining that the most significant criteria for success and advancement are in terms of fine and gross motor skills, how well they draw or use scissors, we are missing the most important part of receiving the Kingdom as a child (Mark 10:13-16). Jesus was referring to the tender hearts of children who have no difficulty understanding their dependence and need for parental care and instruction.[10]

Children should be taught from an early age that part of maturing into adulthood is to discover those unique gifts that God *has* placed within them and that concomitant with these gifts come duties and responsibilities.

---

10   I've seen more than a few homeschooling moms torture themselves because they use these artificial standards to assess themselves as teachers and their children as students. When they buy into the idea that success for their children lies in the categories of what they can do rather than who they are there is often undue heartache and distress.

Recognizing them as Individuals

My son, from the time he was little, demonstrated entrepreneurial tendencies. When we would have discussions about him making his bed, he informed me that he was going to invent a machine that would handle this chore he disliked so much. When we discussed the practicality of such a device, he then told me that if he couldn't make one, he would have to make sufficient money to pay people to do this for him. By listening to him and relating to him as someone who was entitled to his likes and dislikes, throughout his growing-up years, I was able to understand how he was oriented and could always incentivize his behavior by a system of rewards that fit his personality. His competitive spirit could always be counted on to play a prominent role in any endeavor he undertook. So, when I wanted him to memorize Scripture or the Westminster Shorter Catechism, I arranged for a meaningful prize to accompany the accomplishment.

My youngest child, fourteen years her brother's junior, entered our family well into our homeschooling journey. The tendency for me was to assume she'd react and relate to incentives as had her older brother and sister. She was not entrepreneurial as her brother, nor as strong-willed as her sister. She did manifest some obvious musical gifts and an empathetic spirit very early on. The mistake I made at the outset was to assume I could deal with her just as I had done with the other two. By eventually viewing her as the individual she is, with definite strengths and weakness, I was better able to provide the guidance that my job as her mother required. Neither her age nor her size was any reason to try to bulldoze her into adhering to false standards of accomplishment. Patience and God's road map (His unchanging law applied to parenting) helped me prioritize what things I should emphasize regularly and what I could make of secondary emphasis. I stopped majoring in the minors and placed her relationship to God as a top priority.

Rushdoony states,

> [O]ur lives and our schooling cannot be for our pleasure or profit, but for the glory of God …
>
> [T]he focus of education is not on the child, nor on the parents, nor on society. It is on God. Education is thus pri-

marily theological, God-centered, not vocation-centered nor knowledge-centered. Because of the Biblical doctrine of calling or vocation, the Christian School will strive to excel all others in preparing its pupils, but the focus will be on our necessary service to God. Because God's revelations give knowledge, and because knowledge is an aspect of God's image in us, we will seek to surpass all other schools in this respect also. Our focus, however, will be on the competent and faithful service of God.[11]

ETERNITY IN THEIR HEARTS

Ecclesiastes 3:11 says, "He has made everything beautiful in its time. Also, He has put eternity in their hearts, except that no one can find out the work that God does from beginning to end."

It is precisely by recognizing that children are eternal beings and that they have no less a standing in God's eyes just because of their size or age, that we can guide them into paths of righteousness. Thus a mother's privileged role is to steward the life of her child, acknowledging from the outset of their relationship that her child is made in God's image and that His creative efforts will manifest and are to be developed.

When adults speak to children, it should be with these realities in mind. The personhood of all children (from the moment of conception onward) is such an important doctrine for our day. Devaluing the life of the child in the womb has served to devalue children in general, often classifying them as burdens or trophies or slaves of a tyrannical state, but certainly not as the eternal beings they are. If we wish to reverse this revolt against maturity, here is a place to begin.

---

11   R. J. Rushdoony, *The Philosophy of the Christian Curriculum* (Vallecito, CA: Ross House Books, [1981] 2001), 142.

10

A Mother's Nose

My nearsightedness can be easily be traced to my father, whose myopia was genetically passed on to me. It has been said that if a person is deficient in one of his senses, the other ones are sometimes amplified to make up for it. Well, that may explain why I have a heightened olfactory sense. Just recently this "gift" was driving me crazy.

There was an awful smell in my kitchen. I repeatedly brought my husband and daughter into the room to see if they smelled it. Both initially said "no," but eventually said that maybe they smelled something. I even brought another person in to see if he smelled it. His conclusion, "You have a very good sense of smell, but I don't smell anything."

I tried to identify the source of the odor. I thoroughly cleaned the kitchen, sanitized the garbage disposal, and removed potential culprits. Nothing seemed to work and after a while the smell disappeared. Then a couple of days ago, the house was filled with a swarm of small flies that made me feel like a ninja because they were so easy to swat. (Normally, I fail in achieving a successful swat!)

A Google search led me to the conclusion that what I had smelled may have been an animal that had died and was decomposing in the wall or under the house. The appearance of the flies, suggested my Google counselors, was evidence of that. It was encouraging to know that we could swat the flies and they would be gone before long. And, they were.

I share this story because it points to another sense of "smell" that a hands-on mom has regarding her children. A mother has a sense of when something isn't quite right with one of her children. Others may not see it and even dismiss her concerns. But, a diligent mom will continue to investigate and work to unearth the problem. While she may never get to the root, there may be evidence that her suspicions are accurate—"flies" may show up to confirm her sense that more was going on than what others could see.

I believe all mothers have the capacity to relate to their children this way, but they lose it or fail to develop it if they are not the main person raising the child. So many things can go undetected if there isn't a sense of what is "normal" for a particular child. Assuming that child psychologists and their disciples know more than she, and deferring to their expertise, only lessens this God-given instinct and causes a mom not to trust what she senses when others don't agree.

Proverbs 1:7–9 states,

> *The fear of the LORD is the beginning of knowledge: but fools despise wisdom and instruction. My son, hear the instruction of thy father, and forsake not the law of thy mother: For they shall be an ornament of grace unto thy head, and chains about thy neck.*

The mother's role is to know the Law of God and to establish it as the law of her household. When she notices a "bad smell," she needs to get to the root of where and how God's law is being violated or misapplied. The Scripture gives her this responsibility and when exercised in a godly way results in her family's acknowledgements of her inestimable worth.

> *Her children arise up, and call her blessed; her husband also, and he praiseth her. Many daughters have done virtuously, but thou excellest them all. (Proverbs 31:28–29)*

II

Are You Ready?

But sanctify the Lord God in your hearts: and be ready always to give an answer to every man that asketh you a reason of the hope that is in you with meekness and fear. (1 Peter 3:15)

In my time as an active homeschooling parent, my children reported "cross-examinations" by some adults regarding my qualifications as a home educator. My girls were not at a loss regarding how to respond, because they were prepared with a ready answer.[1] The same was true when, because of a flexible schedule, we were out and about during regular school hours. Rather than dread potential questions, we were ready to give an answer suitable to the circumstances and the persons making inquiry.

As homeschooling is still not a mainstream activity, many contemplating removing their children from state schools are fearful of being challenged about their decision and avoid potential detractors. What if, instead, they were eager for the interaction and had a ready answer in place?

I believe we have limited the admonition in 1 Peter 3:15 strictly to theological arguments with atheists or unbelievers, and dismissed (or avoided) opportunities to explain our choices or actions at a more personal level. In any and all circumstances, we need to be prepared to live out and teach that the law-word of God is applicable to all areas of life and thought, and we should be ready to give an explanation as

---

[1]   It always amused them that there was no routine grilling of students in state schools about their teachers' qualifications.

to how this is true. Where we shop, where we vacation, how we pursue recreation, all should connect to the Great Commission (Matt. 28:18–20) and our call to be salt and light (Matt. 5:13–16).

I cannot think of a better goal for any homeschooling mother than to be able to attest that she prepared her children to be ready always with answers to both mundane and abstract questions of life. If a child cannot give a ready answer, the mother must teach him how to discover the answer. So, for the child who is repeatedly questioned about not being with other children, a ready answer might include, "Oh, I have plenty of interaction with other kids my age at church, karate lessons, ballet class, or just spending time with other homeschooling families and people in my neighborhood." You'd be amazed at the effect on adults when a young person, looking them squarely in the eye, provides an answer in a respectful, unflustered fashion. It usually bolsters the case for homeschooling!

How Do You Know What You Don't Know?

Although many begin the process of Christian homeschooling with godly motives, those motives are often incomplete or misguided. Because parents are, themselves, often products of statist education, they don't have a clear concept of how to make their homeschool environment different from the public school alternative.

For example, when I speak to forlorn homeschooling moms about the troubles they are having, the complaints usually come in the form of, "I cannot get her to finish her math," or "He doesn't really want to answer the questions at the end of the textbook chapter." In other words, they are having procedural issues with their children. More obvious (at least to me) is that they have merely taken the public schooling mindset and relocated it to their kitchen table. And why shouldn't they? They have not yet acquired a truly Biblical philosophy of education. They've been to the homeschooling conventions, visited the exhibit halls, and have become convinced Christian education is all about getting the right books (complete with teacher's manuals) and following them exactly. In an effort to justify their educational choice, they load up with materials, and have inadvertently become slaves to the very educational system they are trying to avoid.

Parents need to know what the statist model truly is and why it should not be emulated.[2] If they are unable to make this apologetic to themselves, how will they deal with their children when they encounter resistance, stubbornness, and rebellion?

A Case in Point

A friend contacted me recently about a young mother of three who was struggling with her decision to homeschool. She was seriously considering sending her oldest child back to public school. I was asked to give her a call. After playing "phone tag" for a couple of days, we finally connected. I asked her to tell me what was going on.

She explained that she was finding it difficult to get through all the lesson plans for the various subjects she covered on a daily basis. There were times when her daughter's reluctance frustrated her and she was ready to give up on the process entirely. Additionally, she was concerned that she wasn't giving enough time to her younger children. She told me, in no uncertain terms, that the reason she was homeschooling was because she felt obligated to—that she would never have started if her daughter's previous public school experience had not been so bad. The list of exactly how bad wasn't short! The tone in her voice when she said "obligated" indicated that she felt embarrassed and ashamed that this was her reason.

When she was through I asked, "Since when is doing something out of obligation a bad thing? You sound as though fulfilling your duty as a mother to properly educate your child is somehow demeaned because obligation is your motive." This woman's attitude is all too prevalent in our culture. Simply put, doing something out of obligation—in this

---

2   Rushdoony's *Messianic Character of American Education, Intellectual Schizophre-nia,* and *The Philosophy of the Christian Curriculum* are good places to start. Sam Blumenfeld's *Revolution through Education* and *Victims of Dick and Jane* cement much of Rushdoony's thesis. In the documentary realm, Colin Gunn's *IndoctriNation* has an excellent segment visually depicting the roots and premises of what we know as public schools.

case responding to God's call on her life—was of lesser value than doing something because of an inherent love for the activity.

When I made further inquiry, I discovered that her reluctant student was all of five years old and she was being subjected to a syllabus that was overly academic and tedious. I assured her that for a five year old, she needed to concentrate on Biblical character training, phonics, and basic arithmetic. Additionally, spending time reading to her children, encouraging discussion, and filling their days in exploration of God's world would be far more advantageous than trying to fulfill the expectations of curriculum designers and lots of "seat work." Most importantly, I let her know that her struggles were evidence that she was the one who needed more training.

THE THREE R's

Why are reading, writing, and arithmetic important? If parents cannot give "a ready answer" to this question from a Biblical worldview, they have failed the directive in 1 Peter 3:5. Rather than dreading the questions of their children, their family, friends, neighbors, and members of their church as to why they've taken this unconventional route of home education, they should (along with teaching the basics) prepare themselves to be the best apologists for family-based Christian education. Without a firm mission statement and goal in place, how will they know if (when) they've deviated from their initial path or even arrived at their destination?

That is why homeschooling parents need to spend as much time educating themselves as they do their children. It won't work successfully any other way. In the long run, whether or not someone can diagram an English sentence, translate entire passages of Cicero from Latin to English, generate flawless geometric proofs, be able to describe in detail the process of photosynthesis, or tout a high SAT grade will not demonstrate their qualifications as a godly husband or wife. These will not be good indicators of integrity, honesty, and perseverance. If the focus remains fixed on academic achievements alone, in isolation from godly character development, whatever successes result will not necessarily produce dominion-oriented Kingdom builders.

Since we are all products of our culture and our upbringing, we have to evaluate all our premises and perspectives through the lens of Scripture. While this is a straightforward task, it is not necessarily easy to accomplish, especially when the persons in need of training are busy trying to train their children. This would seem to indicate that the modern practice of extensive professional teacher training prior to placement in a teaching position is superior. Quite the contrary! The most important thing that anyone has to teach is to glorify God by loving Him and keeping His commandments. This task should not be placed in the hands of anyone who is not fully committed to this goal.

In *Intellectual Schizophrenia*, R. J. Rushdoony relates the story of an Armenian mother who took her son to school and entrusted him to the teacher with these words, "His flesh is yours, but the bones are mine." He pointed out that there was a double significance in these words. First, the teacher was given authority to teach and discipline, keeping in mind that the child belonged to the parents, who were delegating their authority. Second, the flesh of the child was to be molded (either by instruction or correction) as necessary, but the basic structure remained with the parents. Rushdoony commented:

> Such education, while often seriously faulty, had a still healthy premise in that it did not assume the right to *re-make* the child, but rather sought to develop him in terms of the family's and society's culture. Modern education is increasingly careless of the flesh but claims the bones of the child, i.e., the right to re-create the child in its own image. When the school is given the flesh but not the bones, the school serves as a cultural agency and limits its function to education. When the school claims the bones, it declares that right belongs to the school and pre-empts the function of home and church.[3]

---

3   R. J. Rushdoony, *Intellectual Schizophrenia* (Vallecito, CA: Ross House Books, [1961] 2002) 133–4.

Parents have the duel function in a homeschooling setting to deal with both the flesh and the bones of their children.

Rushdoony has this to say,

> The sovereignty of God in education requires us to reorganize all education in terms of Biblical faith and presuppositions, to assert the crown rights of King Jesus in every area of life and thought, and to yield unto our Lord His due obedience in church, state, school, home, vocation, and in all of life. Nothing short of this is Christian. The doctrine of God's sovereignty requires it.[4]

Too much of what has been categorized as Christian education has failed to meet this standard. The answer, especially in homeschool settings, is for parents, themselves, to become *better teachers!*

TEACHER TRAINING

> *Call to me and I will answer you, and will tell you great and hidden things that you have not known. (Jer. 33:3 ESV)*

God has promised wisdom to those who seek Him and learn and follow His word. The very same steps that enable someone to become a faithful servant of Christ are required to be a good teacher. A teacher of any subject or discipline must make a self-conscious decision to present the content with the primary, active intent to demonstrate how the student uses the knowledge acquired to glorify God. Many of the women I mentor express concerns that there is so much that they do not know. Their desire to provide a true godly, discipleship education for their children is outweighed (in their minds) by their lack of theological training. They are quite surprised when I offer (as part of the Chalcedon Teacher Training Institute) to help them become theo-

---

4   R. J. Rushdoony, *The Philosophy of the Christian Curriculum* (Vallecito, CA: Ross House Books, 1981, 2001), 115.

logically educated. When I share with them how to get started, they are amazed with how easy Chalcedon has made it for them to begin.[5]

In the end, being able to think, speak, and act in a deliberately Biblical fashion is a life-long pursuit. So there never comes a point when a teacher has *learned enough*. Rushdoony, in his chapter "The Teacher As Student" has this to say:

> Learning involves, among other things, discipline, a desire to learn, and communication. We cannot give others a desire to learn if we do not have it. Most good teachers enjoy studying. A teacher can teach pupils how to read, but a love of reading comes in part from a teacher who shares it ...
>
> The teacher who does not grow in his knowledge of his subject, its methodology and content, is a very limited teacher, and his pupils are "under-privileged" learners ...
>
> Our teaching must be well organized and systematic; if we ourselves are not prone to being orderly in our thinking, our teaching will not be so. Thus, the superior teacher is always disciplining himself in order to pass on disciplined learning to his pupils.[6]

And that is why teacher training needs to be an ongoing task for the home educating parent. Whereas it is somewhat easy to stay ahead of students in their earliest stages of learning, when children reach the point where they are doing extensive reading on their own and formulating questions, only a prepared teacher will be able to infuse a Biblical perspective into her answers. Unless you constantly upgrade your own understanding about current issues in light of Scriptural mandates, you will not be able to give your students the necessary tools so they can *always be ready*.

The Holy Spirit is the teacher of "all truth." Only those who by the Spirit know Christ as Lord of their salvation

---

5   Visit *www.ctti.org*. This program is tailored to individuals and/or groups who wish to make a concerted effort to be the best teachers for their children with an on-the-job training mindset.

6   R. J. Rushdoony, *The Philosophy of the Christian Curriculum* (Vallecito, CA: Ross House Books, [1981] 2001), 132–4.

can know Him as the Creator, and the Lord of all arts, sciences, and learning.[7]

Getting Ready

O how love I thy law! it is my meditation all the day. Thou through thy commandments hast made me wiser than mine enemies: for they are ever with me. I have more understanding than all my teachers: for thy testimonies are my meditation. (Psalm 119:97–98)

As a teacher, nothing is more gratifying than witnessing when your students *get it*. What a privilege it is to be present when your time, efforts, and prayers result in their thinking Biblically and putting legs to their faith (3 John 1:4).[8] Remember that you cannot impart what you do not possess. So, rather than lament your perceived inadequacies, learn alongside your children. The best cure for *inability* is *acquiring ability*. By making the objective to understand all areas of life and thought through the glasses of Scripture, you can't help but impart that to your pupils.

Remembering that the goal is to raise up a generation *ready to give an answer for the hope that is within them*, it is good to be reminded that:

Children are a God-given inheritance for our conquest of the world for Christ. They are a means of subduing the earth and exercising dominion under the Lord. If we give our children to state or private schools which are not systematically Christian in all their curriculum, we are then giving the future to God's enemies, and He will hold us accountable for laying waste our heritage. We thus must

---

7   Ibid., 135.
8   Now that I am no longer actively homeschooling, I experience this with the women I mentor. There comes that point where I know that they have turned the corner and are thinking Biblically.

have Christian schools and Christian homeschools for the Lord's children. We are commanded to "bring them up in the nurture and the admonition of the LORD" (Eph. 6:4). This is a necessary step for that great consummation of God's will, announced beforehand for us in Revelation 11:15:

> *The kingdoms of this world are become the king-doms of our LORD, and of his Christ; and he shall reign for ever and ever.*[9]

---

9   R. J. Rushdoony, *In His Service* (Vallecito, CA: Ross House Books, 2009), 20.

Appendix

Important Considerations for Expecting Parents

BY JO LOOMIS, PH.D.[1]

*C*hristian parents want the best for their children. When they are expecting a baby, they are full of anticipation, and they pick out just the right name, shop for the layette, paint the nursery, and even begin a savings fund for the child.

But many women today do not plan for the birth process of their child, leaving that to the "experts." There is a trend in this country, in this current generation, not to feel the need to prepare, learn, study, and seek out options for a good birth for the child and mother. But there is no part of a child's life that is not under the loving hand of God; He has planned out the life of this child from the very beginning. Jeremiah 1:5 declares, "Before I formed you in the womb I knew you, and before you were born I consecrated you" (NASB). Psalm 139:13 concurs, "For You formed my inward parts; You wove me in my mother's womb" (NASB). Shouldn't parents take as much care in planning for the birth as they do for the child's future education?

Hollywood and popular television programming portray birth as a very fast and extremely painful process with women screaming in anguish. The truth about the quality and nature of pain in childbirth

---

[1] Dr. Loomis' doctorate is in Nursing Practice. She is a registered nurse, a certified nurse practitioner, and a professor at the University of San Francisco's School of Nursing where she is also the Family Nurse Practitioner Program Coordinator.

is much less dramatic and probably wouldn't sell as many sensational programs. If most of what a woman believes about childbirth comes from these sources, she will be convinced that the only way to survive childbirth is to have as much pain medication as is "safe" and hope for the best. Women have believed that lie for generations with disastrous results in terms of the health and well-being of their babies and their own bodies.

Many women do not know the details of the history of childbirth in this country. Perhaps if they did, they would make better choices as to how their babies and their bodies are cared for during childbirth.

Until the early part of the twentieth century, most births in the United States, as elsewhere around the world, occurred at home just as they had since Eve gave birth to her first child. Women in labor and during birth were attended by female relatives and often a midwife, which means "with woman." Today, a midwife is a health care professional educated and trained to provide prenatal, labor, delivery, and postpartum care for a healthy woman who is having a baby. Midwives are fully equipped to handle most common birth emergencies and know when they need to refer to a surgeon. For most women, pregnancy is not a disease, and childbirth is not a dangerous journey. A woman's body is designed by its Creator to work very well during the development of the baby in her womb and during childbirth, which is a normal physiological process.

Similarly, breastfeeding is a relatively new word in our culture. A few generations ago, a baby would simply be fed immediately after birth as part of its usual care, and only the absence or extreme illness of the mother would require artificial feedings. Yet today both a woman's body and her God-designed means of feeding her baby are considered defective and require a specialist's intervention for a safe passage. It wasn't always that way.

Before the early decades of the last century, most women wouldn't even think about having their babies with a physician, much less in a hospital. Hospitals were considered a place to go if there was no other hope, a place to die.

For royalty, childbirth was another matter. These women were attended by their own private physicians. Queen Victoria used chloroform for pain relief during the birth of her third and subsequent babies. This became a symbol of status, and more women began to demand medications for pain during labor and delivery, requiring the move from home to hospital and the need to be under a physician's care. Gradually, it became a sign of prestige and wealth to be accompanied by a physician for childbirth. During this time physicians worked to discredit and eventually disenfranchise midwives.[2] Even today the public is largely unaware that the claims made against midwives are largely untrue.

Deaths related to pregnancy and childbirth dropped drastically in the United States from the late 1930s to the mid 1980s.[3] This change has been heralded as a triumph of medical science as the move was made from the home to the hospital. However, tremendous strides in the standard of living, such as improved sanitation, better housing and working conditions, improved diet, and more widespread health education are more likely causes of these improvements.[4] This was happening all over the industrialized world.

Even so, rates for disease and death during childbirth, both for mother and baby, were higher in the United States than for many other industrialized countries. According to a study in the 1920s, more mothers and babies died in hospitals than at home with births attended by midwives. A closer examination of the statistics reveals that a larger percentage of those who died were upper class and wealthier women as opposed to the poorer women. The women who could afford to be attended by physicians also suffered more medically unnecessary interference with the normal labor and delivery process.

In fact, a national study published in 1932 concludes:

> That untrained midwives approach and trained midwives surpass the record of physicians in normal deliveries has been ascribed to several factors. Chief among these is the fact that the circumstances of modern practice induce many physicians to employ procedures which are calcu-

---

2   American Association for Study and Prevention of Infant Mortality Transactions of the First Annual Meeting. Johns Hopkins University, Baltimore, November 9–11, 1910; Neal Devitt, "The Statistical Case for the Elimination of the Midwife: Fact versus Prejudice, 1890–1935," *Women and Health*, Vol. 4, 1 (1979): 81–96.

3   Donna L. Hoyert, *Maternal Mortality and Related Concepts*, National Center for Health Statistics. Vital Health Stat 3(33) (2007).

4   Irvine Loudon, "Maternal Mortality in the Past and Its Relevance to Developing Countries Today," *American Journal of Clinical Nutrition* (2000), 72, 241S–6S.

lated to hasten delivery, but which sometimes result harmfully to mother and child. On her part, the midwife is not permitted to and does not employ such procedures. She waits patiently and lets nature take its course.[5]

Obstetricians are surgeons who are trained in pathology and trained to care for the abnormal in pregnancy and childbirth. These physicians in the early part of the twentieth century felt that labor was a dangerous passage and required specialized care. They often used medical procedures and instruments to speed up labor and delivery. Many times these caused harm to the mother or the baby, and a large percentage of infant deaths during this time were a result of birth injuries.[6]

A colorful example of this dichotomy is the story of Mary Breckinridge and her Frontier Nursing Service in the Appalachians in Kentucky. During the 1920s and 1930s this mountainous area of the United States was one of the most impoverished in the country. Many areas were accessible only by horseback. Mrs. Breckinridge trained nurse midwives to provide basic prenatal care and nursing services to poor women who otherwise would have no care during childbirth. Her remarkable improvements in the health and well-being of mothers and infants in this poor, rural area surpassed those in hospitals in the nearby cities and across the entire United States, achieving about ten times lower rates of maternal death related to childbirth.[7]

Just before World War II, there was a significant drop in the rates of death and illness of mothers and babies with the introduction of the class of antibiotics called sulfonamides, which prevented deaths from puerperal fever.[8] (Back in the 1840s physicians had a much higher rate of patients with this deadly infection, commonly called "childbed fever," than did midwives, even under the same hospital roof:

---

5   Louis S. Reed, *The Costs of Medicine: Midwives, Chiropodists, and Optometrists* (Chicago: University of Chicago Press, 1932).

6   American Association for Study and Prevention of Infant Mortality. First Annual Meeting, Baltimore, Maryland. November 9–11, 1910; W. Seeley, "The Effects of Interference in Obstetrical Cases." Read before the Child Hygiene Section of the American Public Health Association at the Fifty-Third Annual Meeting at Detroit, Michigan, October 21, 1924.

7   Loudon, "Maternal Mortality," 243S.

8   Ibid.

midwives washed their hands before examining a woman in labor and performed fewer vaginal exams overall.) Later, with the introduction of penicillin and better obstetric care, the rates of death and disease for mothers and babies dropped even further.

During the 1940s and 1950s women demanded the ability to receive a medication called "Twilight Sleep," a combination of morphine and scopolamine that dulled pain and left the woman with no memory of the childbirth. Women labored alone, without husband or other women for support, and were often tied to the bed so they wouldn't jump out and break their teeth on the edge of the metal bed under the hallucinogenic effects of the drugs. Some of this medication crossed the placental barrier to affect the baby, leaving it sleepy and with breathing and feeding difficulties. Babies were taken to separate nurseries to be fed scientifically developed formula and cared for by nurses until their mothers were free of the drugs and healed enough to care for themselves, often several days or even weeks after birth.

An article appeared in the 1958 *Ladies' Home Journal* entitled "Cruelty in Maternity Wards," describing inhumane treatment of women while medicated in labor.[9] During this time there was a public outcry and reforms were instituted. Today, well into the twenty-first century, concerns are still being raised about the treatment of women and infants during labor and delivery and the use of medications to eliminate pain in childbirth.[10]

The American Society for Psychoprophylaxis in Obstetrics (ASPO) was formed in 1960, whose goal was to educate women to be better prepared for better birth outcomes and healthier babies. Later this organization became Lamaze International.[11]

Also in the 1960s, electronic fetal monitoring was introduced, and it is commonly used today. Yet fifty years later there are no quality studies that show the effectiveness of its routine use.[12] Add to that the frequent use of epidural anesthesia, the frequent augmentation or

---

9   Gladys Denny Schultz, "Cruelty in Maternity Wards," *Ladies' Home Journal*, May 1958, 44–45, 152–155.

10 Henci Goer, "Cruelty in Maternity Wards: Fifty Years Later," *The Journal of Perinatal Education*, 19 (3), 33–42.

11 Judith Lothian and Charlotte DeVries, *The Official Lamaze Guide: Giving Birth With Confidence*, 2nd ed. (Minnetonka, MN: Meadowbrook Press, 2010), 16.

12 P. Steer, "Has Electronic Fetal Heart Rate Monitoring Made a Difference?" *Seminars in Fetal & Neonatal Medicine*, February 2008, 13(1): 2–7 (34 ref).

induction of labor with an artificial oxytocin (Pitocin), and 33 percent cesarean-section rates climbing to nearly one in every two childbirths in some hospital settings, and birth in this country has become anything but "normal."

We are told that these are best care practices, yet with some of the most expensive medical care in the world, the United States has worse pregnancy outcomes than most of her industrialized neighbors, coming in at a ranking of forty-first in maternal deaths, according to the World Health Organization.[13] California recently reported an increase in maternal deaths that may partially be due to the increase in elective C-sections performed there.[14]

In countries where birth is treated as a normal, natural process, and where it is attended mostly by midwives, birth is safer with less risk of death or damage to mother and baby. That is much of the rest of the industrialized world. Yet America, as a formerly Christian nation that has been blessed with tremendous medical and technological advances in the past few decades, treats pregnant women and their children as if the marvelous creation of the woman's body is defective and needs highly specialized interventions and interference to function.

Christian parents must wake up and recognize that without arming themselves with the truth about the process of childbirth, and by submitting to these interferences ignorantly, they are exposing both baby and mother to potentially life-threatening dangers. When choosing a birthplace for their child and a professional to attend the birth, couples should ask questions about the risks and benefits to the mother and baby for every intervention and option. The birth of the child, as well as the child's later care and education, belong firmly in the control of the parents.

---

13   "Women and Health: Today's Evidence, Tomorrow's Agenda," World Health Organization, November 2009, http://whqlibdoc.who.int/publications/2009/9789241563857_eng.pdf

14   Nathanael Johnson, "It's Now More Dangerous to Give Birth in California Than It Is in Kuwait or Bosnia," *California Watch*, February 2, 2010, http://www.alternet.org/investigations/145524/df

Index

CPSIA information can be obtained at www.ICGtesting.com
Printed in the USA
BVOW040515221012

303430BV00005B/5/P